Foundations History

BRITAIN 1750–1900

Susan Willoughby

Heinemann

Heinemann Educational Publishers
Halley Court, Jordan Hill, Oxford OX2 8EJ
a division of Reed Educational & Professional Publishing Ltd
OXFORD MELBOURNE AUCKLAND
CHICAGO PORTSMOUTH (NH) BLANTYRE
IBADAN GABORONE JOHANNESBURG

First published 1992

This edition published 1995

99 10 9 8 7 6 5

**British Library Cataloguing in Publication Data is available
from the British Library on request.**

ISBN 0–435–31687–7

Designed by Ron Kamen, Green Door Design Ltd, Basingstoke

Illustrated by Barry Atkinson, Jeff Edwards,
Andrew Greenwood, Douglas Hall and Peter Hicks

Printed in Hong Kong by Wing King Tong Co. Ltd.

The front cover shows an election in Covent Garden in 1818.

Acknowledgements

The author and publisher would like to thank the following for
permission to reproduce photographs:

Agricultural Economics Unit, Oxford: 2.2D
Avon Reference Library / Rob Cousins: 2.14C
Bodleian Library: 1.1D, 4.3C
Bridgeman Art Library: 1.1H, 2.6A, 2.9B, 2.11B, 2.13B, 3.4C,
4.5A, 4.6C, 5.1A
Bridgeman Art Library / British Library: 3.2B, 3.6J
Bridgeman Art Library / Fitzwilliam Museum, University of
Cambridge: 1.1E
Bridgeman Art Library / Gavin Graham Gallery, London: 2.16Z
Bridgeman Art Library / House of Commons: 1.1C
Bridgeman Art Library / Royal Holloway and Bedford New
College: Cover, 2.12C, 2.16T
Bristol Museum and Art Gallery: 3.1A
British Library: 1.1F, 3.5D
British Museum: 4.1B, 4.2B
Celtic Picture Library: 2.4C
Communist Party Picture Library: 4.8J, 4.8P
Corcoran Gallery of Art, Washington DC: 3.3A
Edifice / Adrienne Hart-Davis: 5.2
Edifice / Lewis: 5.2
E.T. Archive: 4.2C
Mary Evans Picture Library: 2.1E, 2.12B, 2.13D, 2.14A, 3.2E,
3.6H, 4.7D, 4.8B, 4.8C, 4.8I
Giraudon / Bridgeman Art Library: 4.1C
Guildhall Library / Bridgeman Art Library: 1.1B, 2.9C, 2.12A,
2.14B
Her Majesty the Queen: Cover
Michael Holford: 2.8A
Michael Holford / Science Museum, London: 2.14D
Holt Studios International: 5.2
Hulton Deutsch Collection: 2.16Q, 3.6R

Illustrated London News Picture Library: 3.4B
Institute of Agricultural History and Museum of English Rural
Life: 2.2H, 2.3C
Leeds City Council, Department of Leisure Libraries: 2.16B,
2.16E
London Transport Museum: 5.1B
Mansell Collection: 1.1G, 2.5A, 2.5C, 2.5D, 2.7C, 2.10C,
2.16L, 2.16Z, 4.2D, 4.4E, 4.8G
Merthyr Tydfil Library Service: 2.16J
Metropolitan Museum of Art, New York: 2.6D
Museum of London: 2.10B, 4.3B
National Maritime Museum, London: 3.6D
National Maritime Museum, San Francisco: 2.13A
National Monuments Record: 2.16K
National Museums and Galleries on Merseyside: 2.2G, 2.7A
National Museum of Wales: 2.4A
National Portrait Gallery: 1.1A
Natural History Museum, London: 4.6F
Out of the West Publishing / Linda Mackie Collection: 2.3B
Picturepoint: 3.2D
Punch Library: 4.5B, 4.7F, 4.8O
Quadrant Picture Library: 2.13E, 5.2
Science Museum, London: 2.4D
Science and Society Picture Library: 2.16F
Skyscan: 5.2
Tate Gallery, London: 4.6G
Trustees of the Wedgwood Museum, Barlaston, Staffordshire:
2.8B, 3.6P
Trade Union Congress: 4.4C
Victoria and Albert Museum, London: 3.2C
Weidenfeld and Nicolson Ltd: 4.7E, 4.8L

Every effort has been made to contact copyright holders of
material published in this book. Any omissions will be
rectified in subsequent printings if notice is given to the
publisher.

We would also like to thank HarperCollins Ltd for permission
to use Source A on page 10, which was taken from *Agriculture
1730–1872* by J. R. S. Whiting, originally published by Evans
Brothers, 1971.

Details of written sources
In some sources the wording or sentence structure has been
simplified to ensure that the source is accessible.

R. J. Cootes, *Britain Since 1700*, Longman, 1968: 4.3D
C. P. Hill, *A Survey of British History*, Arnold, 1968: 4.3E
Simon Mason, *Transport and Communication 1750–1980*,
Blackwell, 1985: 2.13C
Peter Mathias, *The First Industrial Revolution*, Methuen, 1969:
2.1C
Trevor May, *An Economic and Social History of Great Britain
1760–1970*, Longman, 1987: 2.13F
Charlotte and Denis Plimmer, 'Black Ivory', an article in *The
British Empire*, (Volume 4), BBC / Time Life Books, 1971:
3.6B, 3.6C, 3.6G
Bob Rees and Marika Sherwood, *Black Peoples of the Americas*,
Heinemann, 1992: 3.6I
D. Richards and J. W. Hunt, *Modern Britain 1783–1964*,
Longman, 1965: 3.2A
Dorothy Thompson, *The Chartists*, Wildwood House, 1986:
4.8F
Cecil Woodham-Smith, *The Reason Why*, Heinemann, 1971:
3.4A

CONTENTS

1.1 Britain in 1750

Who ruled Britain ?

By 1750 **Parliament** had become as important as the king or queen. This change began when Charles I fought Parliament in the English Civil War. Then, in 1688, Parliament asked **William** and **Mary** to come to Britain. This gave Parliament more power. Between 1750 and 1900 two **monarchs** reigned for a long time: George III (1760–1820) and Queen Victoria (1837–1901). They were able to play a part in ruling Britain. But more changes were to take place between 1750 and 1900:

1750: There were very few voters.	**1832, 1867, 1884**: The number of voters grew.
1750: Voters could be bribed.	**1872**: Voting was made secret.
1750: MPs were landowners.	**1892**: Keir Hardie became the first working-class MP.

By 1900 Parliament had become **more powerful** than the king or queen.

King George III (1760–1820). He spent more time helping to run the country than his father had, so he was more popular.

A cartoon showing an election speech. There was no secret voting in the 18th century. Voters were bribed by people who wanted to be MPs.

SOURCE

A painting of Charles James Fox, a famous MP, speaking in Parliament.

A bigger Britain

Britain had been growing since the Middle Ages. First Wales, then Scotland had been added to England to make Great Britain in 1707. But between 1750 and 1900 Britain grew even more. In 1801 Ireland was added to make up the **United Kingdom**.

An empire overseas

Britain had also been gaining lands overseas. This was often as a result of warfare.

- **1757:** land began to be taken in India.
- **1763:** land began to be taken in Canada.
- **1770:** land was taken in Australia.

Little change at home by 1750

Everyday life in Britain changed very little at first. Most people were very poor farm labourers. A small number of rich families owned most of the land, which they farmed or rented out.

D

SOURCE

Farm workers from the time in their working clothes.

Towns in 1750

Most towns were either market towns or ports. They were very small. People who lived in them were mostly craftsmen making goods and clothes for people to buy. London was by far the biggest town. Wealthy families had town houses in London and also in spa towns like Bath. They enjoyed being seen in fashionable places. But the poor parts of towns were dirty and unhealthy. Drunkenness was common amongst the poor.

Changes

This book is about how Britain changed between 1750 and 1900. Life changed a lot after 1750. Methods of farming changed. More and more people went to live in towns. There they worked hard in **factories**. The rich got richer. The poor were still very poor. The changes caused a lot of problems. It took a long time for the government to accept that it must help to solve these problems.

SOURCE

The wealthy Braddyll family, painted in 1789, by Sir Joshua Reynolds.

SOURCE

A picture showing a shop where spirits (drinks like gin and brandy) were sold by the glass. It was drawn in the 1700s.

A painting of rich people enjoying themselves, dancing at the Ranelagh pleasure gardens in London. It was painted in the 1760s.

H

This painting, from 1787, shows people with bad teeth being given new teeth. The teeth came from people who had died in battle or in hospital.

Questions

1 Write down two headings: **Britain in 1750** and **Britain in 1900**.

2 Work through the pages in this unit.
   a Under the first heading make a list of things about Britain in 1750.
   b Under the second heading make a list of the things that had changed by 1900.

3 Underline in one colour the things to do with **government**. In another colour underline the things to do with **making money**.

2.1 Population

Between 1750 and 1901, the number of people in Britain grew so fast that historians have called it a population 'explosion'.

Population in Britain.

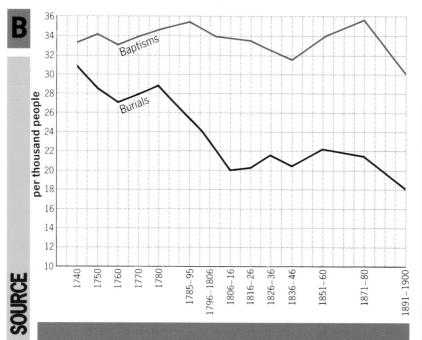

1701 — 5
1801 — 10.5
1851 — 21
1901 — 37

The most important reason why the population grew was that more babies were born and did not die. Also, more people recovered when they were sick because medical care was better.

From 'Freedom and Revolution', by R.J. Unstead, 1972.

Baptisms

Burials

per thousand people

1740, 1750, 1760, 1770, 1780, 1785–95, 1796–1806, 1806–16, 1816–26, 1826–36, 1836–46, 1851–60, 1871–80, 1891–1900

Church records were used to draw this graph of births and deaths between 1740 and 1900. They may be wrong.

It is not true that fewer people were dying after 1780. The Church records are wrong. Not all births and deaths were written down.

Changes in medicine did not make things better. It was because people got married younger and had more children.

From 'The First Industrial Nation', by Peter Mathias, 1969.

The population of Birmingham has increased a great deal. Why?

Because people are having more children. They know that they can send the children out to work to earn money.

Written by Arthur Young in 1774. Young wrote about how people lived at the time.

A cartoon drawn in 1802. Edward Jenner said his 'cowpox' vaccination would stop people dying of smallpox. Many people, like the cartoonist, were scared of the idea.

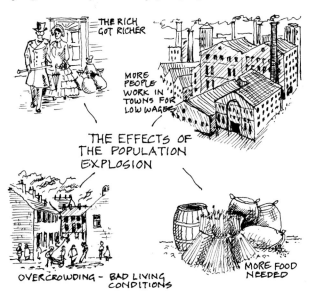

THE RICH GOT RICHER

MORE PEOPLE WORK IN TOWNS FOR LOW WAGES

THE EFFECTS OF THE POPULATION EXPLOSION

OVERCROWDING - BAD LIVING CONDITIONS

MORE FOOD NEEDED

The population after 1880

After 1880 the population stopped growing as fast. People had fewer children. New discoveries in medicine saved more lives. Towns had drains and sewers. This made them better places to live in.

Questions

Look at all the sources.

1 Copy the sentences below. Fill in the gaps.

   a Source A says the population increase was caused by _____.

   b Source B shows the increase was caused by a fall in deaths and a rise in _____.

   c Source C says that it was because _____.

   d Source D says the increase in Birmingham was caused by _____.

Look at the diagram on this page.

2 a Which people did well when the population grew?

   b Which people did badly when the population grew?

2.2 The Agricultural Revolution

Farming in Britain had not changed for hundreds of years. People farmed the 'open' fields around their villages. These fields were divided into lots of narrow strips. Everyone had to grow the same things: wheat or barley. From about 1750, things began to change. They had to. The population was going up, so farmers needed to grow more food.

What was wrong with the old methods of farming?

1 Weeds spread easily across the strips.
2 Land was not used because one field was left empty (fallow) each year.
3 Farmers were not free to do what they wanted with their land.
4 Farmers wasted time travelling between their different strips. They were too far apart.

Why did some farmers want to change?

I WANT TO MAKE MORE MONEY

I WANT TO TRY NEW IDEAS

I WANT MY LAND ALL TOGETHER, IT WILL SAVE TIME

I NEED TO GROW MORE FOOD

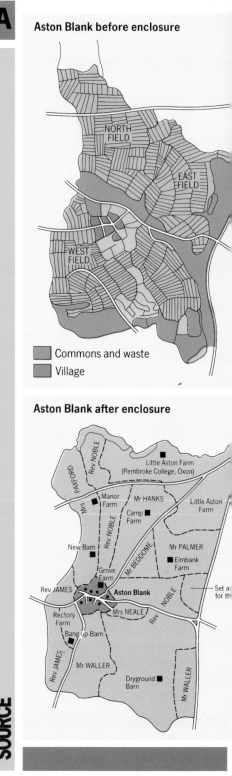

Aston Blank before enclosure

NORTH FIELD

EAST FIELD

WEST FIELD

Commons and waste
Village

Aston Blank after enclosure

Rev NOBLE
Mrs PAXFORD
Rev NOBLE
Little Aston Farm (Pembroke College, Oxon)
Manor Farm
Mr HANKS
Little Aston Farm
Camp Farm
New Barn
Rev NOBLE
Mr BEDDOME
Mr PALMER
Elmbank Farm
Grove Farm
Rev JAMES
Aston Blank
Rev NOBLE
Set a for th
Rectory Farm
Mrs NEALE
Bang up Barn
Rev JAMES
Mr WALLER
Dryground Barn
Mr WALLER

SOURCE

The village of Aston Blank in 1752, bef
and after the fields were enclosed.

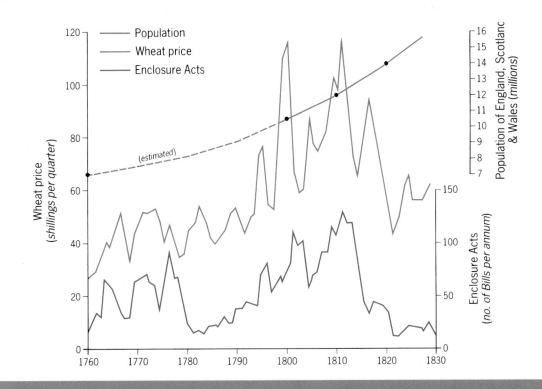

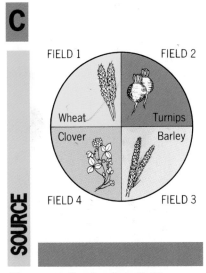

Enclosing the land by order of parliament

Farmers saw that enclosing the land would solve many problems. They made the open fields into enclosed (hedged or fenced) fields. Each enclosed field was made up of lots of the old strips. A different farmer used each field. This meant no travelling from strip to strip. People could only enclose land if parliament said they could. If most people in a village wanted enclosure, parliament could pass a law to force the rest to do it. Between 1760 and 1829 parliament passed 3,670 Enclosure Acts. Even common land was enclosed.

New ideas in farming:

Jethro Tull's Seed Drill planted seeds in straight rows and covered them over. This saved a lot of time.

Viscount 'Turnip' Townshend used turnips and clover to put goodness into the soil. The crops in a field changed each year for four years (see Source C).

Robert Bakewell and the Colling brothers produced new, bigger, breeds of cattle and sheep.

George III and Thomas Coke used the new ideas and methods on their own land. Other farmers saw how well they worked, so they used them too.

When the population grew, there were more people needing food. Prices went up. Farmers enclosed more land to grow more food and make more money.

C

SOURCE

The crops in the four fields on this farm were grown in a different field each year.

Good times, bad times

Farmers did well as long as they could sell their food cheaper than food that was imported (brought in from abroad). The fortunes of farmers rose and fell in the 18th and 19th centuries.

War!

From 1793–1815, Britain was at war with France. No cheap food could come from abroad. This was a good time for farmers.

Peace

Britain and France made peace in 1815. Cheap food began to come into Britain again from abroad. It was harder for British farmers to make money.

The Golden Age of Farming 1840–1870

This was the best time for British farmers.

1 Even more food was needed.
2 After 1850 there were steam-powered machines which helped with the hard work.
3 Marshy land was drained so that more crops could be grown.
4 Fertilizers were used to produce more food.

 SOURCE E

1750	15m quarters
1790	19m quarters
1820	25m quarters

Wheat output in England and Wales between 1750 and 1820. A quarter is about 12.5 kilograms.

SOURCE F

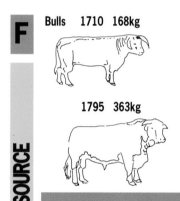

Bulls   1710   168kg

1795   363kg

Average weights of bulls sold at Smithfield meat market in 1710 and 1795.

SOURCE D

Sheep painted in 1866. The artist has made them look bigger.

SOURCE G

A Lincolnshire bull, painted in 1790.

H

SOURCE

A steam threshing machine, drawn in 1860. It separated the seed-corn from the straw. Farm workers had to do this before.

The price of progress

Some people did very well from the changes in farming. Others did not. Enclosure and better farming methods meant there was more food. But some farmers could not afford to use the new methods. Their prices were too high, so they could not sell the food they grew. They had to sell their farms. Many became farm workers instead. Enclosure, and later the new machines, put many people out of work.

Questions

Read **What was wrong with the old methods of farming?**
Look at **Why did some farmers want to change?**

1 Design a poster to show how the new farming is better.
Try to show:
- what was wrong with the old system.
- what was good about the new system.

2 Copy the sentence below that gives the right meaning of 'enclosure'.

Enclosure is fencing lots of strips into one big field.

Enclosure is building homes.

2.3 Agricultural Depression

The Golden Age came to an end in the 1870s. There were several years of bad weather. Crops rotted in the fields. Animals got sick and died. British farmers lost money.

Food from far away places

To make matters worse, food from other parts of the world was being sold in Britain. Steamships brought cheap wheat from North America. Cheaper wool came from New Zealand and Australia. Cheaper meat was brought, frozen, from New Zealand, Australia and Argentina. People bought the cheaper goods. British farmers lost more money. Even more farm workers lost their jobs.

A August was a bad month.

Cattle were stuck in wet pasture. Crops were spoilt. Farmers had nothing to sell.

Instead, people bought cheap American wheat and frozen foreign beef.

SOURCE

From the official farming records for 1879.

B

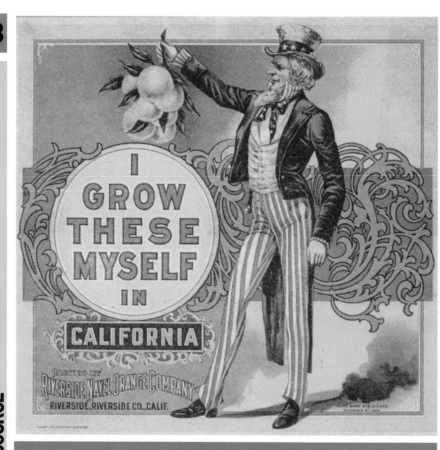

SOURCE

A label from an American orange box, from about 1898.

C

SOURCE

Loading strawberries on to a train going to London in 1906.

A time for change

Farmers had to grow different crops. Some farmers changed to selling milk and butter, cheese and eggs. Other farmers grew fruit, flowers and vegetables. Other farmers sold chickens. The railways carried all these fresh foods to market. Some farmers were helped by this but not all.

Question

Copy out the flow chart below. Put one **cause** (what makes something happen) of farmers losing money in each box on the left. Put one **consequence** (what happens because of something) of farmers losing money in each box on the left.

CAUSES   CONSEQUENCES

D

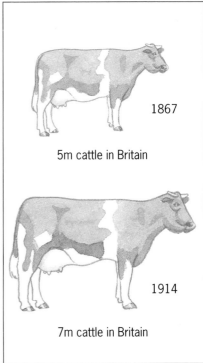

1867

5m cattle in Britain

1914

7m cattle in Britain

1867

1.4 hectares of wheat in Britain

1914

0.7 hectares of wheat in Britain

SOURCE

Changes in agricultural output.

2.4 Power

Sources of power

HORSE POWER

WIND POWER

WATER POWER

A SOURCE

A coalmine in 1786. Horse power is being used to lift the coal.

B SOURCE

May 29: The warm, dry weather is a problem. There is not enough water to power our looms.

August 28: Work has stopped in thirty mills in Blackburn until it rains again.

Written in a Lancashire weaver's diary.

C SOURCE

The watermill at Rossett, Clwyd.

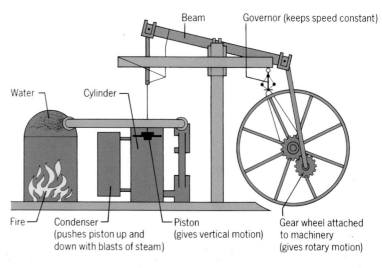

Beam

Governor (keeps speed constant)

Water

Cylinder

Fire

Condenser (pushes piston up and down with blasts of steam)

Piston (gives vertical motion)

Gear wheel attached to machinery (gives rotary motion)

This diagram shows how the Bolton and Watt steam engine (shown in Source D) worked.

Questions

1 Look at **Sources of Power**. Read Source B.
  a What problem might wind power have?
  b What problem might water power have?
  c What problem might horsepower have?

2 Draw the Boulton and Watt engine. Write down two reasons why it was better than earlier sorts of power.

Steam power

The first steam engines were invented by Thomas Savery (1698) and Thomas Newcomen (1712). These engines were used in Cornish tin mines and in coalmines. They were slow and kept breaking down. They could only be used to pump water out of the mines because they only moved up and down.

James Watt

In 1763, James Watt made an even better engine. It was faster, more reliable and used less coal.

In 1773, Watt and his partner, Matthew Boulton, designed a steam engine that could turn a wheel. This is called 'rotary motion'. It was a very important discovery. Steam power could now be used to drive machinery. Steam power was much faster than water, or a horse. It did not depend on the weather, like a windmill. It led to the changes that we call the Industrial Revolution.

D *A steam engine designed by James Watt in 1788.*

SOURCE

2.5 Textiles

Industry in the home

Woollen cloth-making was an old industry in 1750. Cloth was made in the home. Women and children spun the yarn. Men wove it into cloth. It was a slow process.

As the population grew, more cloth was needed. It had to be made quickly and cheaply.

Cotton arrives

Cotton was brought to Britain mostly from America. The cotton industry grew in Lancashire. Cotton was cheaper than wool so it became more popular. New machines made it possible to produce more cloth.

Wool was spun in the home like this before spinning machines were invented.

Inventors and inventions

 1733
KAY'S
'Flying Shuttle'

Made weaving quicker.

 1765
HARGREAVE'S
'Spinning Jenny'
Spun more threads at a time.

1769
ARKWRIGHT'S
'Water Frame'.

Spinning machine. Water powered. For factories only.

1779
CROMPTON'S
'Mule'
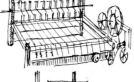
Improved type of 'Water Frame'. Water, then steam powered.

1785
CARTWRIGHT'S
'Power Loom'.
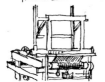
Steam powered weaving machine. For factories only.

Mr Ashton employs 1500 men and women.

400 people work in one big room full of looms.

They pay 3s a week rent for a house on a long street.

From a report written in about 1840.

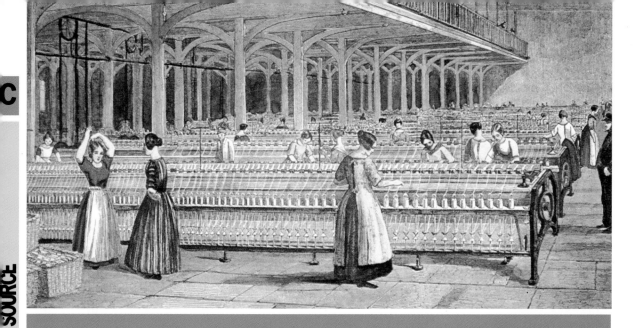

Women using spinning mules in a cotton factory.

From home to factory

The new machines changed people's lives. The machines got bigger. Then they were driven by water power. They could not be used in the home! So cotton spinning mills were built. The workers were mostly women and children, because they could be paid less money. By 1850 the machines in the mills were steam-powered. Mill towns grew up near coal fields, because coal was needed to make the steam. Soon cotton replaced wool as the most important cloth industry.

Questions

1 Make a timeline that runs from 1760 to 1790.

2 Make a list of the machines that were invented in the following years:
1765
1779
1769
1733
1785

3 Put these machines on to your timeline, in the order they were invented.

4 Mark on your timeline when people began to work in factories.

Cheapside

The Cloth Hall, Leeds, in 1813. Merchants are buying and selling woollen cloth.

2.6 Iron and Steel

Iron was one of Britain's oldest industries. Iron works were set up mostly in areas where there was iron ore and a lot of woodland. Charcoal (burned wood) was used in iron making to smelt (melt) the iron ore.

A new demand for iron

In the 18th and 19th centuries, the demand for iron grew. There were more people needing fire grates and cooking pots. Iron was also used to make many of the new inventions that were changing Britain. It made railway tracks, steam engines, new machines and bridges. Iron was also used to make gates, door knockers and other objects to decorate people's homes.

Better and better

New discoveries made it possible to make good quality metal quite cheaply. Below are some of the most important discoveries.

1709:

Abraham Darby made iron making cheaper.
He used coal made into coke to melt iron ore in huge blast furnaces. Coal was cheaper and more plentiful than wood. Iron making moved to areas where there was iron ore and lots of coal.

1784:

Henry Cort made iron stronger.
His 'puddling process' heated the iron twice.
The liquid metal was stirred in the second heating.
This took away all the gases and impurities.
It made strong iron that could be shaped (wrought iron) cheaply.

1840:

James Nasmyth made a steam-powered hammer.
This beat the impurities out of the iron.

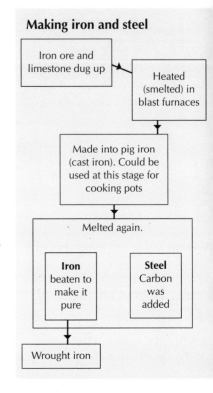

Making iron and steel

Iron ore and limestone dug up → Heated (smelted) in blast furnaces → Made into pig iron (cast iron). Could be used at this stage for cooking pots → Melted again.

Iron beaten to make it pure → Wrought iron

Steel Carbon was added

A painting from 1772. It shows white hot iron being hammered to remove impurities. The big hammer is being powered by a water wheel.

1856:

Henry Bessemer developed a 'converter' at his works in Sheffield. Carbon and manganese were added to the iron while it was a hot liquid. This made a new metal called steel. Steel was a pure, strong metal – stronger than iron.

Iron and steel became very important industries in Britain.

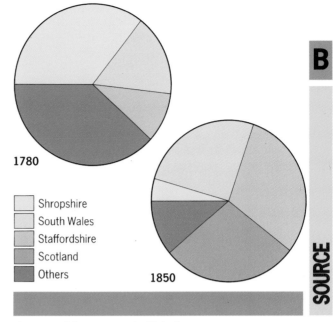

- Shropshire
- South Wales
- Staffordshire
- Scotland
- Others

1780

1850

Iron making areas in Britain.

Questions

Read the second sentence on page 20.
Read **Better and better**.

1 Copy and complete the sentences below:
Before 1709 _____ was used to melt iron ore.
_____ _____ used coke in his blast furnaces to melt iron ore.
_____ _____ invented the process for making steel.

Read **A new demand for iron**.

2 List at least five things that were made of iron at this time.

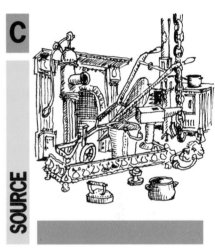

In the 1820s, people wanted everything made of iron!

A painting from 1877. It shows men using a steam hammer. The work was still hard and dangerous.

21

2.7 Coal

Mining in 1750

In 1750 Britain had a lot of coal in many areas (see the map on page 28). Coal was mainly used to heat houses and cook with. Miners did not need to go deep underground to dig out all the coal that was needed.

More coal!

After 1750 there were more homes needing coal. Coal was also needed for blast furnaces and steam engines. So miners had to go deeper underground.

Problems and some solutions

Mining deep underground had problems that early mining did not have. There were many accidents. People had to work hard to find solutions to the problems.

Problems	Solutions
Flooding	Steam driven pumps to remove the water.
Bad air	Trap doors to let air in. Extra shafts (holes) dug to bring in air.
Poisonous gas	Humphrey Davy made his Safety Lamp. The flame changed colour if there was gas in the air.

B

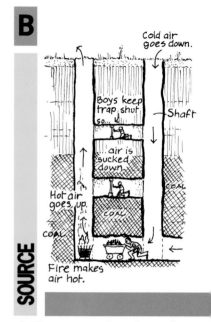

A diagram to show how air was moved around a deep coalmine in the early 19th century.

A scene on the surface of a coalmine. The steam-powered machine in the centre is pumping water out of the mine.

A

Working in the mines

Getting the coal up from the mine was a problem. It was very heavy. Sometimes whole families worked in the mine. The father cut the coal. The mother and children dragged it to the bottom of the shaft. At first, they had to climb up to the top, carrying the coal in baskets.

Later, lifts got the coal up the shafts – not women and children. The lifts were powered by horses and then by steam. Railways took the coal to where it was needed. By 1900, coal was a very important British industry. So much coal was produced that there was even enough to sell to other countries.

The coalfields of Britain, 1800.

Central Scotland

North East

Yorkshire, Derbyshire, Notts.

South Wales

Midlands

C

SOURCE

A painting of a Yorkshire miner. The engine behind him is an early steam-powered wagon.

Questions

Read **Problems and solutions**.
1 Copy the sentences below. Fill in the gaps.

Flooding was solved by using

_____.

Bad air was solved by _____.

People used _____ to find out if there was poisonous gas in the air.

Look at the map on this page.
2 Where was coal mined?

Look at Sources A and C.
3 a What kind of transport is being used in Source A?
   b What kind of transport is being used in Source C?

2.8 An Entrepreneur – Josiah Wedgwood

Entrepreneurs are business people. They buy **raw materials** cheaply and make them into goods. Then they sell them at a **profit**. Business people helped to make Britain a rich, industrial country between 1750 and 1900. Josiah Wedgwood is a good example of a clever and successful entrepreneur. From 1759 his name became famous for china (a very fine kind of pottery). This was carefully made and beautifully decorated in very special styles. Everyone could recognize Wedgwood china.

New ways to make fine china

Josiah made his china in stages. Craftsmen were responsible for each stage:

A blue jasperware trinket box showing neoclassical design; part of Wedgwood's ornamental ware.

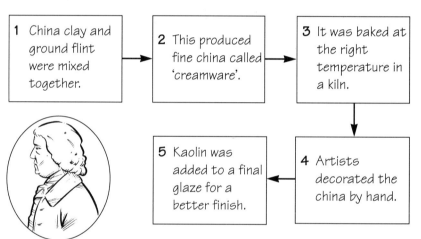

1. China clay and ground flint were mixed together.

2. This produced fine china called 'creamware'.

3. It was baked at the right temperature in a kiln.

5. Kaolin was added to a final glaze for a better finish.

4. Artists decorated the china by hand.

Why did people want china?

Drinking tea and coffee was popular in the 18th century. Well-off people wanted china cups. Wedgwood saw his chance to make money.

Why was he so successful?

Josiah ran his business well.
- He made sure that his pottery was good quality.
- He sent samples to wealthy and important people.
- He sent travelling salesmen around the country.
- He gave money back if customers were not satisfied.
- He gave money to build roads and the Grand Trunk Canal to carry his goods safely.

Wedgwood's London showroom for ornamental and useful ware, 1809.

C

The Duke of Marlborough, Lord Gower, Lord Spencer and others have been to my works. They have bought some china. (**1765**)

I want a large room to show off my ornaments and dishes. The displays can be changed often. (**1767**)

Kings and princes have had my china in their palaces for a long time. Now all the middle classes want to buy them. They will buy a lot if the price is right. (**1771**)

We will still have to pay the same rent and wages even if we only make a small number of pots. So we might as well make a lot and make more money. (**1771**)

Taken from some of the letters of Josiah Wedgwood.

Questions

1 Make a list of the things that were special about Wedgwood's pottery.

2 Make a list of the things that made Wedgwood a good businessman.

3 Design a poster advertising Wedgwood china. Put on it all the things that you think would encourage people to buy it.

2.9 The Industrial Peak?

The 'workshop of the world'

In 1851 Britain made a lot of money from industry and trade. A great deal of money came from making a lot of goods in factories and from trade. Some workers were better paid, so could afford better food. Britain led the world in inventions, and in making the most of them. This made the people of Britain very proud.

The Great Exhibition – 1851

A Great Exhibition was held in London. A special building – the Crystal Palace – was built for the event. It made of glass, with an iron frame. The Exhibition was held to show that Britain led the world in industry. People came from all over Britain and all over the world to see it. Visitors saw the latest factory and farm machines, steam engines and forms of transport. Over half of the exhibits were from Britain. Visitors could see why Britain was rich.

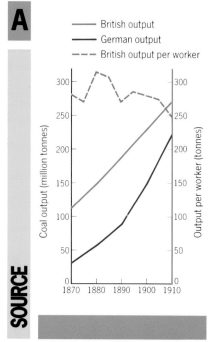

A SOURCE

- British output
- German output
- - - British output per worker

Coal production, 1870–1910.

B SOURCE

A wall painting called 'Iron and Steel'. It was painted in 1861 in Northumberland.

One of the Machinery Halls at the Great Exhibition, drawn in 1851.

Would the good times last?

The Great Exhibition itself made a lot of money for Britain (£186,000). But it also showed Britain's foreign competitors how to be even better. They copied the latest ideas and machines in their factories. Then they thought of better ways for themselves.

Falling behind?

British factories still used earlier inventions. It would cost too much money to keep changing. But some countries, like Germany and the USA, used the new methods. They produced goods more cheaply. More people bought their goods, instead of British goods.

The year 1851 was a special year for Britain. But after 1851, Britain gradually lost its leadership of the world in farming and in industry.

Question

Copy the following sentences in **chronological** order. That is the order they happened.

After 1851 Britain lost the lead in farming and industry.

By 1851 Britain led the world in industry.

The Great Exhibition was held in 1851.

Other countries started to use new inventions, Britain did not.

People came from the USA and Germany to get new ideas.

D Each year, more cotton goods are made in factories in India. This is bad news for the Lancashire cotton mills.

From an article about Lancashire cotton mills, written in 1913.

E No-one else can make motor cars like the Americans.

From the 'Illustrated London News', 1888.

2.10 Transport – Roads

The need for better roads

The coal, iron and cloth industries made more and more goods. These had to be taken all over Britain. They also had to be taken to ports to send abroad. In 1750, Britain's roads were bad. They had to be made firm and strong.

The road-builders

The first really good roads were only made after 1750. The most famous road builders were John Metcalfe, John Macadam and Thomas Telford.

Smooth surface of small stones

Medium sized stones

Sloping road surface to let rain drain away

Good drains at side of road

Large boulders

A cross section of a Telford road.

A SOURCE

Some roads were so wet that they did not even dry out in the summer. The roads were so deep in mud that horses were not strong enough to pull a coach. Oxen had to be used.

A journey round Britain described by Daniel Defoe, in 1724.

A scene in a market town at the time when travelling by road became popular.

B

SOURCE

A painting from 1829. It shows a stagecoach at a toll house.

C **SOURCE**

D **SOURCE**

The road from Salisbury to Romsey is the best. It is straight and wide enough for three carriages. There is a grass verge on each side. It looks in very good condition.

Arthur Young went round England in 1768. He liked the new roads in the south.

The Turnpike Trusts

Groups of businessmen got together as Turnpike Trusts. They paid men like Telford to build roads. These roads were much better. They charged people to use them. Several toll gates were built on the roads. Toll-keepers took the money from travellers on the roads.

The advantages of better roads

Some people did not like paying tolls. But good roads made travel much easier. People could travel more quickly and comfortably, especially by stagecoach.

Questions

Read **The Turnpike Trusts.**

1 Copy the sentences below. Fill in the gaps. Use the words in the box.

Turnpike Trusts hired men like _____ to build new roads. They charged _____ to use the roads. Travellers paid the money to keepers in _____ houses.

toll	Telford	people

Read Source A. Look at the cross section of Telford's road.

2 a Draw a cross section of what you think the road in Source A was like.

   b Draw the cross section of Telford's road next to it.

Look at Sources B and C.

3 List the different people who used the roads.

Water transport

It was much cheaper to carry heavy goods by water than by road. Boats already carried goods round the coast. There were also rivers that boats could sail along. These were called 'navigable' rivers. Not all rivers were deep or wide enough to sail along. In the 18th century, canals were built joining the rivers (see map on this page). So goods could be carried quite long distances along rivers and canals.

Canals and canal builders

The great canal builders were James Brindley and Thomas Telford. The Duke of Bridgewater paid Brindley to build a canal from his coalmine in Worsley to Manchester. Other businessmen had canals built. They then charged others to use them. Some of these canals were:

1757: Sankey Brook Canal

This canal joined St Helens, the River Mersey and Liverpool.

1761: Bridgewater Canal

This canal carried coal from Worsley to Manchester.

1777: Grand Trunk Canal

This canal joined the Rivers Trent and Mersey.

By 1790 the canal network had grown. Aqueducts took canals over rivers. Locks carried canal boats uphill.

A Trade will grow in the North if goods can be sent by water.

The distance will be less than by road. It will cost less. Goods will not be broken.

SOURCE

Written by cloth merchants in Yorkshire in about 1700.

- —— Canals
- —— Navigable rivers
- ▨ Coalfields

Network of canals and navigable rivers in 1830.

A painting of the Regent's Canal, 1827. Canals took grain to London from the countryside.

C

One horse pulling a wagon along a rail can pull 8 tons.
One horse can pull a canal boat and 65 tons.

From a letter to a magazine in 1810. It took 4 horses to move 1 ton on a road at the time.

D

The price of carrying the clay to the pottery will go down a lot.

It will also cost a lot less to carry the pottery to the ports when it is made.

Josiah Wedgwood, talking about the benefits of water transport, in 1765.

Advantages of canals

1 They gave people jobs.
2 They carried heavy goods cheaply.
3 They were good for carrying breakable goods, like pottery and china.

Disadvantages of canals

They were slow. This meant they could not be used to carry goods that went bad or that died quickly.
When there were long spells of hot weather some parts became too shallow and difficult to use.

The biggest problem for the canals was the arrival of a new form of transport that was cheaper and quicker – the railways. The days of canal transport were numbered.

Questions

Read **Canals and canal builders**.
1 Copy the sentences below. Choose one of the words in *italics* each time.
The great canal builders were James *Brindley/Boyle* and Thomas Telford. They were hired by *boys/businessmen*.

2 You are the owner of a canal. Make a poster to get people to use your canal.

2.12 Transport – Railways

Canals were soon replaced by a much cheaper and faster kind of transport – the railways.

The first railways

Railway lines were first used to carry coal from the pithead. The heavy carts were pulled along the tracks by horses, not by steam engines.

Richard Trevithick and William Hedley

In 1804 Richard Trevithick built a steam locomotive that could pull carts. It only ran on a small, round track. Even then, it broke down a lot. Then, in 1813, William Hedley built the 'Puffing Billy'. This was the first engine to pull coal carts. By 1823 there were twenty of these engines in use. But they only travelled short distances.

George Stephenson, 'father of the railways'

In 1821, George Stephenson, an engineer, was asked to find a way to move coal from Stockton to Darlington. In September 1825, Stephenson's steam engine, called 'Locomotion', made the 40 kilometres trip pulling coal wagons and passengers. It was a great success.

A

SOURCE

A picture from 1852. It shows a coach driver in 1832 and a railway engine driver in 1851.

B

SOURCE

Farmers found the railways useful, too.

'The Railway Station', painted in 1862.

The 'Rocket'

Stephenson was employed to build another railway, from Liverpool to Manchester. In 1829 there was a competition to find the best locomotive to run on it. Stephenson's 'Rocket' won easily. The Liverpool to Manchester Railway opened in 1830 carrying goods and passengers.

Mad about railways

The Liverpool to Manchester Railway made a lot of money for its owners. Other people wanted to make money from railways. Soon railways were being built all over Britain. By 1852, there were 10,600 km of track!

The impact of the railways

Good points:

1 They carried goods quickly and cheaply.
2 They made travel quick and easy.
3 They made jobs for people.
4 They helped the iron and coal industries to grow.

Bad points:

1 Some farmers thought that the noise would harm their animals.
2 People worried about the dirt (pollution) and noise.
3 Canal and coach owners could not compete. Railways were quicker and cheaper. So jobs were lost as well as made.
4 The new lines were set up by different companies. They used different widths of track. People had to keep changing trains.

Question

Copy the following sentences in **chronological** order. That is the order they happened.

a In 1830 the Liverpool to Manchester Railway opened.

b In 1804 Richard Trevithick built the first steam locomotive.

c In 1825 George Stephenson's engine pulled passengers and coal wagons for 40km.

d The first engine to pull coal carts was 'Puffing Billy', built in 1813.

2.13 Transport – Britain Overtaken

Sail or steam?

People wanted to cross the oceans quickly to buy and sell goods. Would steam power make ships go faster? The first wooden steamships were slow. They also kept breaking down and could only travel short distances. One of the first wooden steamships was the '**Charlotte Dundas**', built in 1804.

Then, in 1838, two steamships crossed the Atlantic. One was the American ship the '**Sirius**'. The other was British, the '**Great Western**', built by Isambard Kingdom Brunel. Now there were people who began to think that steamships were better than sailing ships. Steamships got bigger and better. Brunel built the '**Great Britain**' in 1843 and the '**Great Eastern**' in 1858. They were made of iron. In 1881, the first steel ship, the '**Servia**', was launched from Scotland.

But some people still believed that sailing ships were best. The American clipper ships, designed in 1845, were fast. They competed with steamships for a while. But they could not solve the problem of how to move the ship quickly if the wind was wrong. By the 1860s everyone accepted that steamships were better.

B

SMALLEST & SHARPEST CLIPPER LO...
Coleman's California Line
FOR SAN FRANCIS...

The A 1 Extreme Clipper Ship
SYREN
GREEN, Commander, is now rapidly Loading at PIER 11,
This beautiful little Clipper has made some of the fastest passages o...
From SAN FRANCISCO to BOSTON, in 100 DA...
From NEW-YORK to SAN FRANCISCO, in 120 DA...
From CALCUTTA to BOSTON, in   96 DA...
always delivering her cargoes IN PERFECT ORDER. Shippers will...
the MOST DESIRABLE VESSEL NOW LOADING. For balance of Freight, ap...
WM. T. COLEMAN & CO., 161 Pearl Str...
Agents at San Francisco, Messrs. W. T. COLEMAN & Co.   N...

SOURCE

A poster from the 1850s. It is advertising an American clipper ship.

C

The Americans could build more wooden ships because there was no shortage of trees.

SOURCE

From 'Transport 1750–1980', by Simon Mason, 1985.

A

SOURCE

An American clipper ship, painted in 1850.

The liner 'SS Ophir' in a port in Egypt in 1900.

Early motor bicycles and cars

People began to try to make vehicles powered by a motor. But early attempts to develop a gas-powered motor were not successful.

At last – the petrol engine!

In Germany, in the early 1880s, Gottlieb Daimler and Karl Benz invented a petrol engine for a car or bicycle. Petrol driven cars were soon on sale in Germany. Britain did not catch up until 1896, when the first British car was made by Fred Lanchester. Rolls Royce began to make cars in 1906.

E

SOURCE

F

SOURCE

Europe led the way in developing the petrol engine. Laws were passed in Britain to stop cars taking the place of coaches and the railways.

From a book written in 1987. A law passed in 1865 said cars could not travel above 4mph. A man with a red flag had to walk in front to warn everyone else on the road!

Questions

1 Read **Sail or steam**? Copy the sentences below. Choose one of the words in *italics* each time.
The first steamships were made of *wood/metal*. They were very *fast/slow*. Most people thought *sail/steam* was best. Then *iron/wood* steamships were made. They crossed the *Atlantic/Black Sea*.

2 You are the captain of a clipper ship in 1845. Draw an advertisement to encourage a trader to use your ship.

A French car factory in about 1898.

2.14 An Engineer – I.K. Brunel

Britain needed **engineers** between 1750 and 1900. They designed roads, canals, locks, bridges, railways and tunnels. This was important work. It helped Britain to become a great industrial country. Brunel is a good example of an engineer at this time.

Isambard Kingdom Brunel was born in 1806 and died in 1859. He designed the **Clifton suspension bridge** in Bristol but he died before it was completed. He left many other things to remind us that he was a clever man.

Railways

In 1833 Brunel was given the job of building the **Great Western Railway**. It ran from London to Bristol. Work began in 1835. It took six years to build and cost £6.5 million. He had to build a tunnel (the Box Tunnel, near Bath) which took over two years to complete. It also cost the lives of 100 workers. Two grand stations were also built: **Paddington** (in London) and **Temple Meads** (in Bristol).

A

SOURCE

Isambard Kingdom Brunel.

B

SOURCE

This is the entrance to the Rotherhithe tunnel. It was built by Brunel and his father to carry road traffic under the river Thames. But it was not deep enough, so water kept breaking through. When it was opened in 1843, it could only be used by pedestrians.

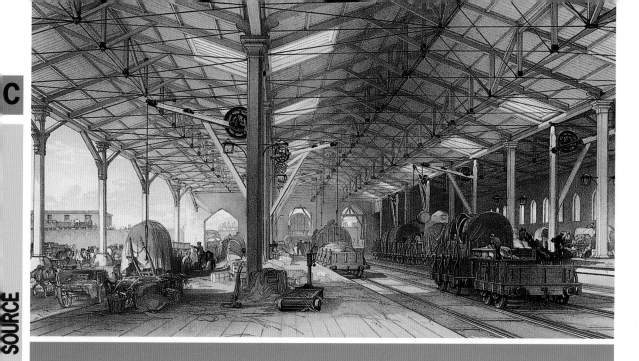

C

SOURCE

The western terminus of the Great Western Railway, Temple Meads Station, at Bristol.

Ships

Brunel also designed three ships.

1 The '**Great Western**' (launched 1838) was a paddle steamer with an oak hull. It weighed 1,320 tons and could cross the Atlantic in fifteen days.

2 The '**Great Britain**' (launched 1843) was the first ship with an iron hull and a screw propeller instead of paddles.

3 The '**Great Eastern**' (launched 1858) weighed 20,000 tons. It was the largest ship in the world with steam powered screw propellers and paddles. It carried 4,000 passengers, 5,000 tons of cargo and used 300 tons of coal a day.

Questions

1 Find out what Brunel did in each of these years:

1835	**1843**
1838	**1858**

2 Read **Railways** and **Ships** and the sources. Complete these sentences:

a I think Brunel's greatest success was _____ because _____ _____.

b I do not think Brunel was completely successful because_____.

D

SOURCE

The 'Great Eastern'. This was a great ship but it was too heavy. It got stuck in mud when it was launched!

2.15 Connections –The Industrial Revolution

The diagram below shows the changes which you have been learning about so far. We call these changes 'The Industrial Revolution'.

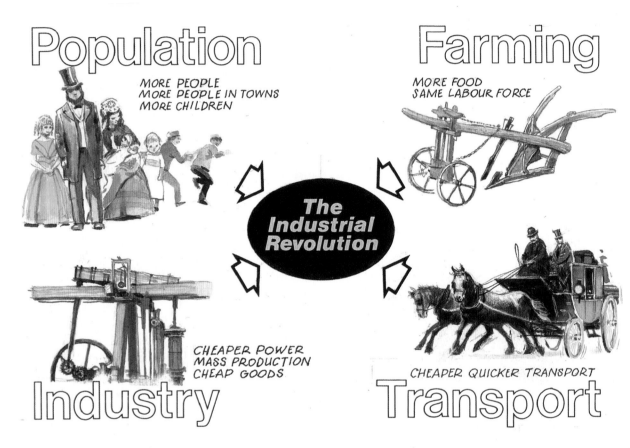

Population
MORE PEOPLE
MORE PEOPLE IN TOWNS
MORE CHILDREN

Farming
MORE FOOD
SAME LABOUR FORCE

The Industrial Revolution

Industry
CHEAPER POWER
MASS PRODUCTION
CHEAP GOODS

Transport
CHEAPER QUICKER TRANSPORT

This diagram shows the changes as being separate. But really they are linked. Changes in one could not have happened without the others. Look at the chart below.

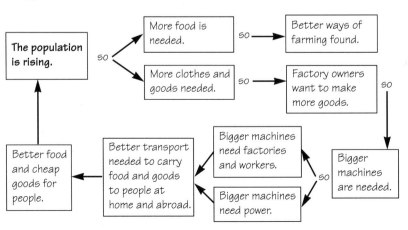

The population is rising. → so → More food is needed. → so → Better ways of farming found.

so → More clothes and goods needed. → so → Factory owners want to make more goods. → so →

Bigger machines are needed. → so → Bigger machines need factories and workers. / Bigger machines need power. → Better transport needed to carry food and goods to people at home and abroad. → Better food and cheap goods for people. →

Questions

1 Copy out the second diagram.

2 Choose **three** colours. Shade in different colours the boxes that are about **farming**, **transport** and **industry**.

The diagram below is another way of showing the changes that we call the Industrial Revolution. Again the changes are in **population**, **farming**, **industry** and **transport**. They are all joined together by a whirlwind.

Industrial Britain 1900

Britain in 1750
(before the Industrial Revolution)

Question

Do you think that a whirlwind is a good way of showing the Industrial Revolution?

2.16 Life and Work in the Towns: A Study in Depth

The coming of industry changed the way people lived and worked. Here you can learn more about living and working in towns.

How towns grew

After 1750 the population grew very fast. Factory towns grew especially quickly. So factory owners had to build homes for their workers.

Sewage, water and waste

Houses were built very quickly wherever there was space. They had no clean, running water. Lots of families shared these houses. This made them overcrowded. Often 30 or 40 families shared one toilet!

Sewage ran out into the street and into nearby rivers. Most families got their drinking water from the same rivers. If they wanted clean water they had to buy it. Rotting rubbish piled up in the streets. There was no one to take it away. The smell was terrible.

A SOURCE

Year	Population
1801	53,000
1811	62,000
1821	83,000
1831	123,000
1841	152,000
1851	171,000

The population figures for Leeds, which was a factory town. These figures are taken from the government census (official counting of the people).

A view of Leeds produced in 1715.

B SOURCE

Only 2,200 houses (12,000 people) get clean water from the water works. Sixty thousand people have no water. They have to get it from wells or they drink rainwater.

From a Commercial Directory of Leeds, 1834. This was a book that listed all the streets and businesses in the town.

The worst parts of Leeds are where houses are built around 'yards'. There is no fresh air, drainage or toilets. Where there are toilets, they are open to the street and overflowing. Sewage stands there for six months or more. Rubbish of all kinds is thrown into the street.

From a government report by James Smith, 1845.

Questions

1 Write two headings: **Leeds in 1715** and **Leeds in 1846**. Look at Sources B and E.

2 **a** Write down under each heading the things that are **different**.
 b Write down under each heading the things that are the **same**.

A view of Leeds produced in 1846.

Disease

In these filthy conditions, disease spread very quickly. **Smallpox, typhoid** and **tuberculosis (TB)** were common, especially in poor, overcrowded areas. They were killer diseases. But by far the worst of these killer diseases was **cholera**.

Cholera

Cholera was carried by water, but in the 19th century no one knew this. It spread very fast. People died quickly and in agony. The worst cholera epidemics were in 1831, 1848, 1854 and 1866. Although cholera mainly killed poor people, it also killed the rich. People realized that dirt and disease were connected. So something had to be done.

I

SOURCE

Deaths from Cholera	
Year	Deaths
1831	32,000
1848	62,000
1854	20,000
1866	14,000

Number of deaths caused by cholera epidemics in Britain.

F

SOURCE

A cartoon called 'Monster Soup', drawn in 1828. It shows the cartoonist's views on the dirty state of the river Thames in London.

G

SOURCE

There is a huge dunghill here. The owner sells it. The older the dung, the higher the price. The smell is so bad that people all around have to keep their food covered. It tastes of the dunghill.

A doctor describing Greenock in Scotland. This was for a government report written in 1842, by Edwin Chadwick.

Question

Look at Sources H and I.
Complete these sentences:
People lived longer if they lived in the _____. This was because
_____.
The worst cholera epidemic was in _____.

No.	When taken ill.	When died.	Where died.	Sex.	Age.	Occupation.	Circumstances.	Habits.	Any evidence of contagion or infection.	State of the Dwellings or Neighbourhood.
1	22nd August...	24th August ...	15, David square, Abercannaid	M.	36	Wife of Puddler (Welsh)	Very poor ..	Dirty	No possible contact ...	Damp, dirty, and unventilated.
2	22nd ,, ...	25th ,, ...	57, Quarry row, Tydfil's Well	F.	45	Wife of Fireman ... (Irish)	Poor	Dirty	ditto	Dirty, unventilated—yard at back most filthy.
3	23rd ,, ...	25th ,, ...	31, do do ...	M.	32	Fireman.............. (Welsh)	Good	Clean and regular	ditto ...	A drain, which carries away house slops from houses above, runs under the house.
4	23rd ,, ...	26th ,, ...	13, Morris court, Merthyr	F.	75	Rag cleaner .... (Irish)	Poor	Clean	As a rag cleaner might have picked infected clothes	An untrapped gully at end of court, ash heaps of ashes steeped with excrement, &c. House, no ventilation.
5	24th ,, ...	25th ,, ...	7, Cwm Canol street, Dowlais	M.	21	Hooker in Iron Mills (Irish)	Young Irish Labourer	Regular	No possible contact ...	Cesspool at back of house above level of lower floor—offensive.
6	24th ,, ...	25th ,, ...	1, Flag & Castle ct., Dowlais	M.	8	Son of Labourer ... (English)	Very poor ...	Dirty	ditto	Court unpaved, no convenience, earth sodden with house refuse.
7	24th ,, ..	1st September	16, Sunny Bank, Tydfil's Well	F.	53	Wife of Tailor ...... (Welsh)	Very poor ...	Intemperate & Dirty	ditto	Cesspool in garden overflowing, floor of sleeping room thickly covered with dirt and filth.
8	25th ,, ...	27th August ...	1, Miles' court, Caedraw	F.	50	Wife of Hawker ... (Scotch)	Poor	Clean and regular	Her husband and herself travelled about the neighbouring towns—had been in Aberdare	Cesspool near house overflowing.
9	26th ,, ...	30th ,, ...	8, Coffin's ct., George Town	F.	80	Wife of Skinner ... (Welsh)	Poor	Very clean .	Had attended her son, case No. 3	Unventilated—common cesspool in gardens full.
10	27th ,, ...	1st September	4, Lewis' square, Abercannaid	F.	32	Wife of Collier ...... (Welsh)	Comfortable .	Clean and regular	Apparently spontaneous	Overcrowded with family and lodgers—9 out of the 12 attacked, 7 died. At back of bedroom heap of ashes foul with excrement.
11	28th ,, ...	1st ,, ...	9, Sunny Bank	F.	42	Wife of Labourer ... (Irish)	Comfortable .	Clean	May have visited case No. 7	—
12	3rd September	5th ,, }	13, Mt. Pleasant, { Penydarren ......{	F.	21	Wife and { of Daughter{ Collier } (Welsh)	Comfortable .	Clean	No known contact ...{	Unceiled cow shed under the house in a most filthy state.
13	6th ,, ...	8th ,, }		F.	8					

The official records of some people who died of cholera in Merthyr Tydfil in Wales, in 1866.

Market Court in Kensington, London, in about 1865. There were many houses and yards like this.

Working in towns

Many people went to live in the towns so that they could find work in the factories. Before this they had worked in their own homes. Factory life was very different.

Working in factories

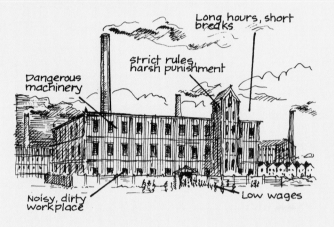

Long hours, short breaks

strict rules, harsh punishment

Dangerous machinery

Noisy, dirty workplace

Low wages

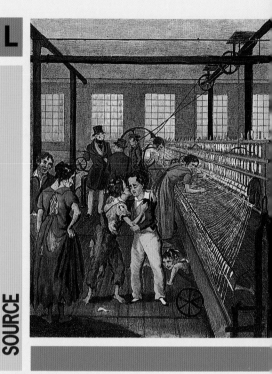

This picture appeared in a novel written by Frances Trollope in 1840. She was strongly against child labour.

At busy times my girls worked 9 hours a day.

They were often beaten with a strap.

They had only 4 hours sleep. On a normal day they were too tired to eat.

My eldest girl lost half her finger in a machine. They would not even pay her wages.

They were paid three shillings [15p] a week and seven pence – half penny [3p] overtime.

Samuel Coulson talks about how his two daughters were treated at work in the mills, in 1832.

N

Girls loved their long hair. So they were sometimes punished by having it cut close to the head.

SOURCE

From a pamphlet about working conditions written in 1837.

O

Children are kicked or cruelly beaten with a horsewhip, strap, stick, hammer or clenched fist.

SOURCE

From a report to Parliament on children at work in 1843.

P

The power loom makes a terrible noise. The man that works on it can be driven mad.

SOURCE

Spoken by a factory worker to some MPs in 1835.

Q

SOURCE

A chimney sweep and boy in the 1860s. Sweeps sent small children up the chimneys to sweep out the soot. They were beaten if they got stuck. Sometimes they died.

R

Sharpening the point on brass pins is a very unhealthy job. There is nothing to stop the worker breathing in the dust of the brass.

SOURCE

A visitor to a Birmingham metal works writing in 1844. This was another kind of job done by people living in towns.

Questions

1 List all the bad things about working in factories.

2 Use your list to make a poster to tell people what is happening to children working in factories. Put as much information on to it as you can.

The poor and paupers

In the 1800s Britain became a rich country. But even by 1900 there were still a lot of poor people. This was because wages were too low. Some workers lost their jobs because of sickness or injury. Then they became **paupers.** Paupers were people who were so poor that they could not take care of themselves and their families without help.

The New Poor Law and the workhouse

Parliament passed a new law in 1834. Parliament wanted to solve the problem of paupers. The law said that those who were old, sick or crippled could be helped at home. But those who were fit enough to work had to go into the **workhouse**. Here, families were separated. The food was poor. Uniforms had to be worn. The rules were harsh. People were punished for bad behaviour.

Poor people waiting for help in the workhouse. This picture was painted in 1874.

Paupers must not:
- use bad language
- make a noise when told to be silent
- refuse to work
- play cards
- insult the officials of the workhouse
- get drunk
- disturb others at prayer.

Paupers will be punished by bein given bread or potatoes instead o a meal. For really bad behaviour they will be put in solitary confinement.

SOURCE

The rules of the workhouse in 1841.

SOURCE

Why were living and working conditions so bad?

You might ask why the factory owners and landlords got away with treating people so badly. People today are protected by laws. They stand up for their rights to proper treatment. Why did none of these things happen in the 19th century? There are several reasons:

1 The government did not think that it was right to interfere in the everyday lives of people – rich or poor. So factory owners were left alone to run their factories. This was known as *laissez-faire*. They were not told to build good houses with clean water supplies either.

2 Many people made a lot of money with things as they were. They did not want this to change.

3 Working people were afraid of losing their jobs. So they did not want the government to pass laws. Many of them chose to send their children to work.

U

SOURCE

It is the duty of the government to protect people and their property. Also to stop crime by making laws and punishing those who break them. It is not the job of the government to help people to look after their families. They must do this for themselves.

From a letter written to the Prime Minister, in 1846.

V

SOURCE

We do not want to be made to have our streets cleaned. We'd rather risk catching cholera than lose our freedom.

From a letter to 'The Times', 1854. It argued against public health reform.

W

SOURCE

If laws are passed to control factory owners, they will not be able to make goods cheaply. They will go out of business.

This was said in 1837, by a factory owner who was worried about the effects of government reforms.

X

SOURCE

The factory owner's profit is made in the last hour of the day. If that hour is taken away by law then he will lose his profit.

This was said in 1837, by a man who studied how money was made.

Y

SOURCE

If children are not allowed to work more than eight or ten hours a day, thousands of families will not have enough money to live on.

From a Leeds newspaper, printed in 1831.

Time for change

From the 1820s, some men began to press the government to accept that it must protect and care for people who could not help themselves. They wanted Parliament to pass laws to **reform** the factories and provide **public health** (clean water, sanitation, better housing) in towns. Reform means to change or reorganize things to make them better.

Who were the reformers?

Robert Owen and **John Fielden** were factory owners. But they treated their workers well. They wanted MPs to realize that all factories could be like theirs.

Richard Oastler drew attention to the ill-treatment of children and the long working hours in factories. He said the factory workers were treated like slaves in the West Indies.

Lord Shaftesbury led these reformers. They wanted a ten hour working day. He also worked hard to stop small children working in factories, coalmines and other workplaces. He said that they should be in school!

Edwin Chadwick set to work to make MPs see the terrible conditions in which working people lived. He wanted to shock them into taking action. He published a report in 1842. But it was really the outbreaks of cholera that made the government act.

Victory for the reformers?

The reformers had a hard struggle. The changes they wanted cost money. So it took a long time for Parliament to take action. But in 1867 working men in towns were given the vote. If MPs wanted to be elected they now had to please working people. The box (opposite) shows some of the reforms which were made by Parliament.

Reforms made by Parliament

1833 Factory Act
No children under 9 years were allowed to work.

1842 Mines Act
No women or children were to work in the mines.

1847 Ten Hours Act
Women and children under 18 years to work no more than 10 hours a day. [The same law was passed for men in 1867.]

1848 Public Health Act
Local councils could spend money, **if they wanted to**, cleaning up their towns.

1875 Public Health Act
Towns **had to have** sewers, clean water supplies, pavements and street lighting.

SOURCE

A painting of Liverpool docks. It shows that by 1887, when it was painted, the dockland streets were paved. They were also clean and well lit.

Slow progress

Change and progress was still slow to come. At first crafty factory owners could dodge the law. The government set up inspectors to make sure that the laws were being obeyed. But many of these were friends of the factory and mine owners. In any case there were not enough of them to check regularly. Parents often lied about the age of their children to keep them at work. Parents wanted to work longer hours themselves. Women wanted to work in the mines.

By 1900 doctors were making new discoveries in medicine. Wages were just about rising faster than prices. But there was still no help for old people. Poverty was a problem. Slum areas remained in many towns.

Question

Look at pages 47 and 48. Suppose you asked each of the following persons if they wanted reform:

- **a factory owner**
- **Richard Oastler**
- **an MP**
- **a factory worker with young children**
- **a pauper**.

Write down what each one might say in reply and why.

3.1 Trade

In 1750 Britain made a lot of money from trade. Ships carried British goods to other countries. They left from the ports of London, Liverpool, Bristol, Glasgow and Hull. They brought back raw materials (things from which more goods are made from, like cotton cloth).

Exports, imports and taxes

Exports are goods that are sold to other countries. **Imports** are goods bought from other countries. To make money countries have to export more than they import. Some goods that Britain imported were also made or grown in Britain. Wheat is a good example. People bought foreign wheat if it was cheaper than British wheat. So, to **protect** British farmers, the government put a tax on foreign wheat. This made foreign wheat more expensive. People then bought British wheat after all.

A scene at the busy port of Bristol in the 18th century. Merchants (traders) made money from trade. This money was used to help new industries to grow. It also helped to improve roads and to build canals and railways.

SOURCE

Trade with the colonies

Britain ruled lands in other parts of the world. For example, the thirteen colonies on the east coast of America. These colonies were not allowed to buy or sell goods to other countries. All goods had to be sent through Britain. This made the Americans very angry. So in 1776 they fought a war against Britain and won (the **American War of Independence**). As a result, Britain lost her colonies in America.

Adam Smith and free trade

In 1776 Adam Smith wrote a book called the *Wealth of Nations*. He said that taxes did not help trade to grow. By 1840 Britain made more goods than any other country. British industries did not need taxes to protect them any more. No one else could make goods cheaper than Britain. No more were taxes put on goods from other countries. This was called **free trade**. Britain sold more goods.

Trade in trouble

Britain's trade boom lasted until about 1870. By that time other countries were developing their industries – especially Germany and the USA. By the end of the 19th century, they were sending cheaper goods to Britain. So British industry needed to be protected once again.

People were worried about Germany producing cheaper goods than Britain.

Questions

Look carefully at Source A.

1 Describe a walk along the docks in the picture. Say what you might hear, see and smell on the docks.

2 Complete these sentences:

The British government had to put taxes on foreign goods because

_____.

After 1840 taxes were taken off because

_____.

C

SOURCE

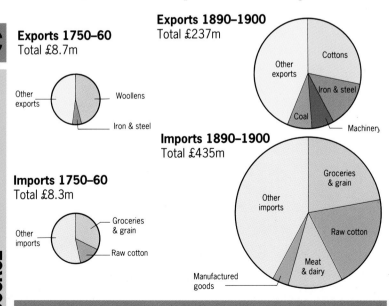

Exports 1750–60
Total £8.7m

Other exports — Woollens — Iron & steel

Exports 1890–1900
Total £237m

Other exports — Cottons — Iron & steel — Coal — Machinery

Imports 1750–60
Total £8.3m

Other imports — Groceries & grain — Raw cotton

Imports 1890–1900
Total £435m

Other imports — Groceries & grain — Raw cotton — Meat & dairy — Manufactured goods

British imports and exports, 1750–1900.

3.2 Empire

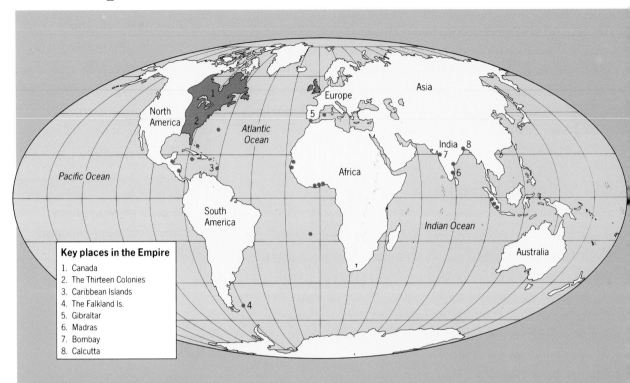

Key places in the Empire

1. Canada
2. The Thirteen Colonies
3. Caribbean Islands
4. The Falkland Is.
5. Gibraltar
6. Madras
7. Bombay
8. Calcutta

The British Empire in 1763.

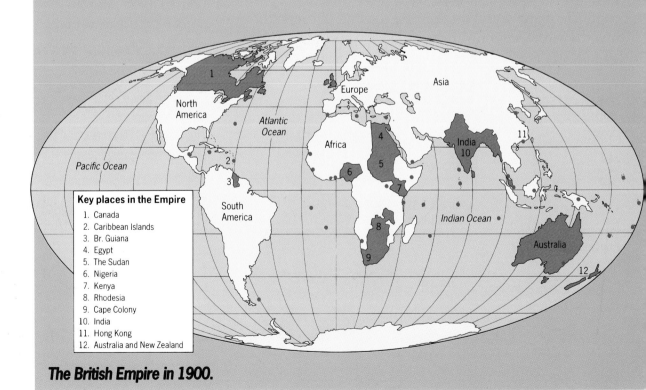

Key places in the Empire

1. Canada
2. Caribbean Islands
3. Br. Guiana
4. Egypt
5. The Sudan
6. Nigeria
7. Kenya
8. Rhodesia
9. Cape Colony
10. India
11. Hong Kong
12. Australia and New Zealand

The British Empire in 1900.

Britain's growing empire

Look at the maps on the opposite page. You can see that, in 1763, the British Empire was quite small. An empire is made up of colonies – land in one country that belongs to another country. Canada, the American colonies and the Caribbean Islands (West Indies) belonged to the British government. The small dots, mostly in India and Africa, show where British companies had set up trading posts.

By 1900, the picture was very different. Britain now owned colonies in Africa, India, Australia and New Zealand as well as Canada. It was the biggest Empire in the world.

Why did Britain want an empire?

1 To buy

From as early as the 17th century, merchants made money by selling foreign goods in Britain. They bought luxury goods cheaply (like silks, spices and gold) in places like the East Indies and India. They sold these goods for a high price in Britain.

2 To get raw materials

Britain's industries grew in the 18th and 19th centuries. The factories needed more raw cotton and other raw materials. The factory owners wanted to buy these as cheaply as possible, to make more money.

3 To sell

The people of the colonies had to buy goods from Britain. So Britain sold more goods.

4 To get power

Countries with an empire were powerful. As the British Empire grew, other countries wanted colonies too. Britain had to take more land to stop others becoming more powerful.

A SOURCE

In 1750, the British people took very little interest in the colonies. They weren't any better off for having them.

From Richards and Hunt, 'Modern Britain 1783–64', written in the 1960s.

A painting from 1823. It shows slaves working on a sugar plantation in the West Indies.

B SOURCE

How did Britain get the Empire?

Britain got different parts of the Empire in different ways. Sometimes the takeover was quick. Sometimes it took a long time. Sometimes part of the Empire broke away again.

1 Settlers

In the 17th century, people left Britain and settled on the east coast of America. They went for many reasons, but mostly to be allowed to follow their own religion. By 1750 there were thirteen colonies in America. Britain ruled the Thirteen Colonies until 1776. Then the Americans fought a war with Britain. They became free to rule themselves in 1783.

2 War

Britain fought France in the 18th century. Britain won, and took Canada and the West Indies from France.

3 Discovery

In 1770 Captain James Cook claimed Australia for Britain. People began to emigrate (go to live and settle) to Australia after about 1852.

4 Trade

The British government slowly took over areas where companies went to trade. India and parts of Africa were added to the Empire in this way.

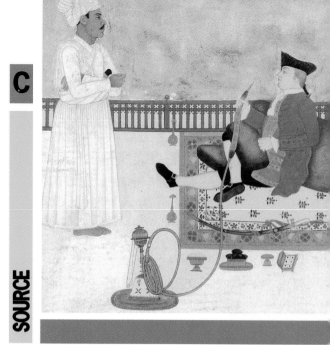

C SOURCE

A painting from 1780. It shows an important employee of the East India Company in 1780. He has an Indian servant. He is smoking, Indian style.

D SOURCE

A 19th century painting of life in Australia. Settlers in Austra took land from, and even hunted, the Aborigines who lived

Good for Britain?

There were ways in which having an empire was very good for Britain. Britain got cheap raw materials. People in the colonies bought British goods. Britain was seen as a great power. But by 1900 cheap food from parts of the Empire was arriving in Britain. British farmers suffered.

Good for the colonies?

Some native people accepted the British. Others did not. The British needed an army to support their rule. The British built roads, railways, schools and hospitals. But not all changes were for the better. The British forced people to use the British language, religion, customs and lifestyle. The culture of the people in the colonies was almost destroyed.

Questions

Look at the maps on page 52.
1 How did the Empire change between 1763 and 1900?

Look at all the sources.
2 a Which sources show that the British treated the local people badly? Explain your choice.
  b Which sources show that the British admired the local people? Explain your choice.

Read **Good for the colonies?**
3 Was it good for the colonies to be part of the Empire?

The Royal Pavilion at Brighton built in about 1820. It was built in the eastern style.

E

SOURCE

3.3 Emigration

Between 1815 and 1900, 13 million people left Britain (emigrated).

Why emigrate?

1 **To escape poverty.** Many working people felt that there was little hope for them in Britain. They lived in bad conditions. They had hardly enough money to buy food. Some were unemployed.

2 **To escape from starvation.** Large numbers of people left Ireland in the 1840s and 1850s. (Look at Source G.) The potato harvests failed in those years. Thousands starved to death. Emigration was their only hope.

3 **To make their fortunes.** Some people went to find gold in Australia or South Africa. Others went because it was their only chance of owning land. They could get cheap (or free) land in Australia, New Zealand or the American West.

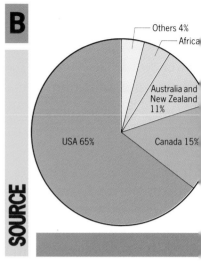

B SOURCE

Others 4%
Africa
Australia and New Zealand 11%
USA 65%
Canada 15%

British emigrants went to these countries 1820–1900.

A SOURCE

A painting of immigrants arriving in New York in 1884. Some immigrants arrived with no money, but died very rich.

C SOURCE

FREE PASSAGE TO AUSTRALIA
Honest, hardworking people wanted.
Farm workers
Miners
Mechanics
Free passage to this healthy country. Workers and their familes sure to find work and a home.

A copy of an advertisement in a newspaper in 1846.

D SOURCE

If boys and girls from the workhouse are sent to Canada, it will help people to get jobs in

From a London magazine, 1866.

Getting there

The government, charities and trade unions all helped the poor to emigrate. People who ran colonies like Australia helped too, because they wanted people to settle there.

Emigrants travelled by railway and steamship. It was a dangerous and unpleasant experience.

E

THE POLITICAL DRAMA.

A cartoon from 1830. The cartoonist thinks the government used emigration to solve all its problems.

F

The voyage lasted for four months. Six or seven people died on the way, mostly children. We had plenty of biscuit to eat, but not much other food. The water was bad. I became very ill. I could hardly walk ashore when we arrived.

From a letter sent by an Australian emigrant in 1849.

G

Decade	Numbers emigrating
1830s	420,000
1840s	1,110,000
1850s	2,054,000
1860s	1,675,000
1870s	1,700,000
1880s	2,900,000
1890s	2,000,000

Emigration from Great Britain in the 19th century.

Questions

Look at Source B.

1 Copy the sentences below.
Fill in the gaps.
Most people went to _____.
The rest went mainly to _____.

Look at Sources C and E.

2 a How does Source C say that emigration would be a good thing ?

b How does Source E show that emigration would be a bad thing ?

3.4 Ireland

Catholics and Protestants

In 1750 the really powerful people in Ireland were all Protestants. They owned almost all of the land. But most of the people in Ireland were Roman Catholics. The land had once belonged to them. Now they had to rent it. This made them angry.

Laws against the Irish Catholics

The British government was afraid that the Irish Catholics would help Britain's enemies. So it did everything it could to make Irish Catholics weak. There were laws which were hard on Irish Catholics. They could not own land. They could not have important jobs in the government or the army. This made the Irish even more angry.

Part of Britain?

In 1798 there was a revolt in Ireland led by Wolfe Tone. The revolt failed. William Pitt, the British Prime Minister, decided that Ireland must become part of Britain. In 1801 parliament passed the Act of Union. But union with Britain did not bring peace. Nothing was done to change the unfair laws that made the Irish angry.

The Great Hunger 1845–49

The poor in Ireland lived on potatoes. Between 1845 and 1849, the weather was so bad that the potato crops rotted away. Thousands of Irish people starved to death. The British government did very little to help. This made the Irish hate the British even more.

A In 1844, almost all of Ireland was farmland. It was split into tiny bits of land.

The people lived in huts made of mud and stone with turf [grass] roofs. The huts had no chimneys or windows. They had no furniture. The animals lived with the people.

SOURCE

From C. W. Smith, 'The Reason Why', 1971.

A picture of people fighting for food during the Potato Famine. It was drawn at the time.

B

SOURCE

SOURCE

C

A painting from 1840. It shows some Irish people making whiskey.

Ireland in revolt

Then, in 1867, there was more violence led by a group called the Fenians. The British Prime Minister, William Gladstone, saw that to get peace they had to make things fairer for the Irish Catholics. In 1870 and 1881, he tried to pass laws to make landlords treat their Irish tenants fairly. It was hard to make people do this. He had very little help from the rest of the government.

By now the Irish had had enough of British rule. They wanted to rule themselves. Gladstone supported this idea of 'Home Rule'. But neither parliament nor the Protestants in Ireland wanted Home Rule. There was no Home Rule, and there was more fighting. Nothing was solved.

Questions

1 Make a timeline using the events below:

1798, Wolf Tone's revolt.
1801, Act of Union.
1845-49, The Potato Famine.
1867, Fenians revolt.
1870, 1881, laws to help Irish.
1900, Home Rule refused.

2 Underline events which made the Irish angry with Britain.

Look at Source A.

3 What tells you that the Irish were very poor?

3.5 Connections – Industrialization, Trade and Empire

In this part of the book you have been learning about the changes in **population**, **emigration**, **trade** and **empire**. You have looked at each one by itself. But really they were all connected. Look at the diagram below. This shows how they were linked together.

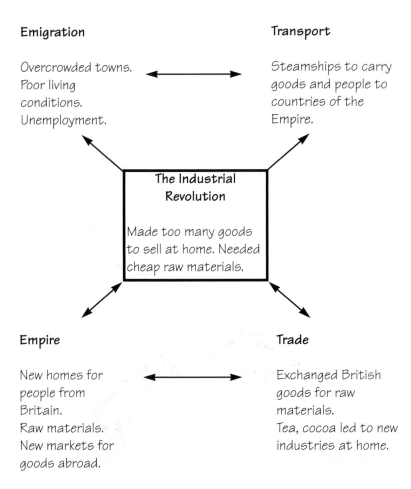

Emigration

Overcrowded towns.
Poor living
conditions.
Unemployment.

Transport

Steamships to carry
goods and people to
countries of the
Empire.

The Industrial Revolution

Made too many goods
to sell at home. Needed
cheap raw materials.

Empire

New homes for
people from
Britain.
Raw materials.
New markets for
goods abroad.

Trade

Exchanged British
goods for raw
materials.
Tea, cocoa led to new
industries at home.

A SOURCE

Yesterday, I went to a meeting of unemployed workers in the East End of London. They were hungry. It made me realize that we need to get new lands where these people can go to live. Then we can send all the extra goods we make for them to buy.

Cecil Rhodes wrote this in 1895. He was a businessman. He helped to make South Africa part of the Empire. He added Rhodesia (now Zimbabwe) to the British Empire.

B SOURCE

'Oh where are you going to, all you Big Steamers,
With England's own coal, up and down the salt seas?'
'We are going to fetch you your bread and your butter,
Your beef, port, and mutton, eggs, apples and cheese.'

An extract from a poem by Rudyard Kipling, 1911.

C SOURCE

A man from Manchester wants somewhere to sell his goods. So he sends a man to make the Africans become Christians. They kill the man. This gives the army an excuse to go and take over.

From 'The Man of Destiny' by George Bernard Shaw, 1898.

A painting showing Robert Clive meeting an Indian prince in 1765. Robert Clive worked for the East India Company.

Questions

1 Copy out the diagram on this page. Draw lines across the circle to show which things are connected. One of these has already been done for you.

2 Complete these sentences:
Steamships helped _____ and _____.
The **Empire** helped **industry** because _____.
New materials such as _____ and _____ helped industry even more.

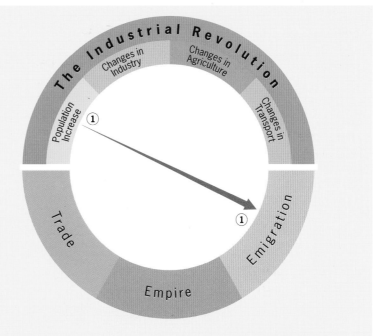

Connection 1 – The growth of population in Britain made cities crowded and caused unemployment. This encouraged emigration.

3.6 The Slave Trade: A Study in Depth

In this depth study of the slave trade you are going to find out the answers to these questions:

- How did the slave trade begin?
- How were the slaves treated?
- How was the slave trade stopped?

Question

Write one or two sentences about the 'Triangular Trade'. Use the map to help you.

What was the slave trade?

British traders bought and sold slaves. They left Liverpool and sailed to West Africa (look at the map). They took cheap goods with them, such as cloth and iron pots. They exchanged these goods for slaves. The slaves were packed on to ships and taken to the West Indies or to America. There they were sold for a very high price. The slave traders made a lot of money. They carried cotton, tobacco and sugar back to Britain.

The Triangular Trade.

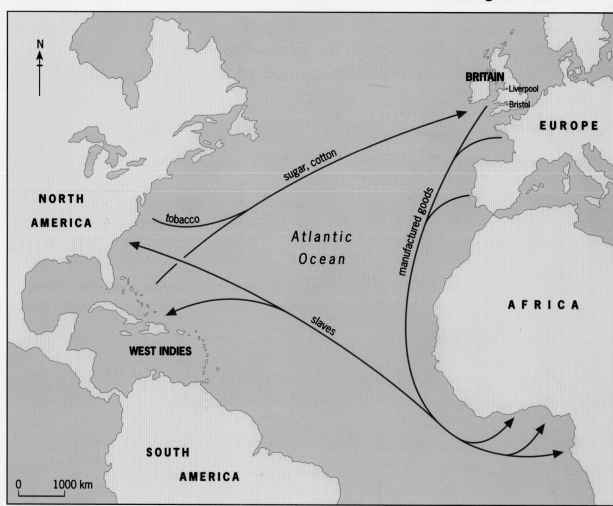

This shows slave traders from Europe unloading their goods on the coast of Africa. It does not really give a true picture of what it was like.

How did the slave trade begin?

From about 1500 settlers from Europe went to America and the West Indies. They set up **colonies** there. They grew sugar, tobacco and cotton on huge areas of land called **plantations**. But these plantations needed a lot of workers. There were not enough white settlers. White settlers could not work for long in the heat. They often became ill. So Spanish traders brought natives from Africa. They sold them to plantation owners. These men, women and children became the property of the owners. They were slaves. They were no longer free to come and go as they pleased.

British slave traders

Some Englishmen also wanted to make money from the slave trade. One of these was John Hawkins (he was the cousin of Francis Drake). He began to sell slaves to Spanish plantation owners in the West Indies in 1562. Soon, Britain was making a lot of money from the slave trade. British ships carried over three million Africans to a life of cruelty and misery in the West Indies and America.

B Britain became a rich industrial country because money from the slave trade was used:

- to build docks, canals and factories.
- to help to build Watt's steam engine.
- to build the Liverpool to Manchester railway.

The view of Charlotte and Denis Plimmer, written in 1971.

How were the slaves treated?

1 Capture

African men, women and children were caught by African chieftains. Some were prisoners of war, some had broken the laws of their tribe. They were sold to slave traders from Europe.

2 The journey – the 'Middle Passage'

Often as many as 700 slaves were packed below the deck of a slave ship (look at Source H). They were chained together. They had to lie on shelves. They had no room to move. It is impossible to imagine the filth and the smell. If slaves became ill, they were thrown into the sea.

When the slaves arrived in the West Indies or America, they were made to look fit and healthy. Then they could be sold for a good price.

C SOURCE

Tribal leaders sold their prisoners of war into slavery. Then they began to sell criminals from their own tribes. Often their crimes were very small. A man and all his family could be sold into slavery.

From a book called 'Black Ivory', written in 1971.

A painting from the early 1800s, showing what it was like below deck on a slave ship.

D SOURCE

E

SOURCE

On board the ship were 336 males and 226 females. They were packed so tightly together that they could not lie down. They did not even have room to move. It was 89°F below deck (32°C).

Captain Newton, describing his slave ship.

F

SOURCE

The slaves had dysentery [this caused terrible sickness and diarrhoea]. There was blood and mucus everywhere. It looked like a slaughterhouse.

Written by a doctor on a slave ship.

G

SOURCE

Sailors were cheap. Slaves were worth a lot of money. So the sailors were treated worse than the slaves. If food was short they weren't fed. They were often flogged. One man jumped overboard because he was flogged so many times.

Another extract from 'Black Ivory', written in 1971.

Questions

Read page 64.
1 Write out this passage, filling in the spaces:
   Slaves came from West _____. They were often _____ or _____ .

Read the sources on page 65.
2 Make a list of the bad things that captains did to:
   a the slaves
   b the sailors.

H

SOURCE

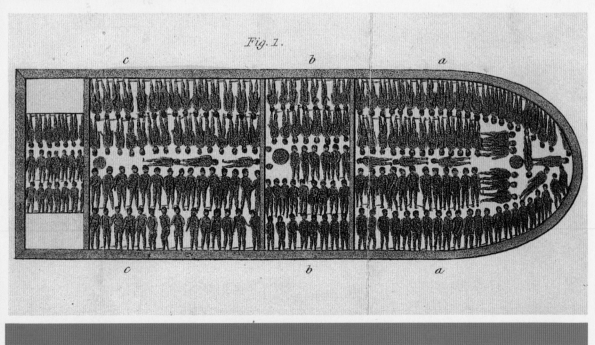

Fig. 1.

This is a plan of a slave ship. It shows the slaves packed together. Slave ship captains had different ideas about this. They did not all carry such large numbers.

3 On the plantations

Slaves were sold on the dockside. They were sold to the people who would pay the most. A strong male slave could fetch about £100. Slaves cost very little to feed and clothe. But their owners made a lot of money from their work.

Many slave owners did not allow their slaves to marry. Male and female slaves were kept apart. Young male slaves were worked to death. Then the owner just bought another. So there was always a demand for slaves. This kept the slave trade going.

Slaves were treated so cruelly that they often tried to escape. Some even killed themselves. Runaway slaves were severely punished (look at Source I).

I

SOURCE

Slaves hated the way the were treated. So they worked slowly, they bro tools and let animals loo They set fire to the house and crops of their owner Owners were even murdered. Punishments included death, whippin or the cutting off of feet, noses or ears.

From a book called 'Black Peoples of the Americas', 1992

Slaves working on a sugar plantation in the West Indies in about 1823.

J

SOURCE

How was the slave trade stopped?

In Britain, there was a long struggle to get the slave trade and slavery stopped altogether.

Support for slavery

People did not know much about Africans. They were disgusted to hear stories that they had many wives and ate human beings. So it did not matter to them if Africans were sold as slaves. As slaves they could become Christians. That made slavery all right!

L

SOURCE

God says that slavery is right, so it is wrong to stop it. It makes the African happy, so it would be cruel to end it.

A Scottish lawyer, writing in 1790.

K

SOURCE

> 792   February 26, 1790.
> # RAN AWAY
> FROM the subscriber, Two NEW NE-GROES, marked I in a diamond on the right shoulder; they are stout men, one about 6 feet high, the other 5 feet 6 or 7 inches. Whoever delivers said negroes to THOMAS WATT, on *Lilliput-Hall Estate*, or W. & J. PATTINSON, *Montego-Bay*, or will lodge them in any Workhouse in this island, shall be handsomely rewarded.
> *JOSEPH JOBLING.*

An advertisement in a newspaper. Notice that the slave has been branded. This showed that he belonged to his owner.

M

SOURCE

The plantation owners do not want to think of their slaves as human beings. They want to treat them as dogs or horses.

Written by a man called Edward Long, in 1774.

N

SOURCE

Africans are not human. If we say that they are human, people will say that we are not Christians [because of the way the slaves were treated].

A French writer and thinker, writing in the 18th century.

O

SOURCE

The slave trade makes Britain rich and powerful. We cannot do without it.

Written in the 18th century by a man who studied money matters.

Question

Read page 67. You are the owner of a sugar plantation. You are told that keeping slaves is wrong. Make a list of the things you might say to defend yourself.

2 The end of the slave trade at last!

In 1787 the Quakers and Evangelicals joined together in the fight against slavery. They formed the **Committee for the Abolition** (banning) **of the Slave Trade**. They started a campaign to tell people how badly slaves were treated. They won a lot of support from important people.

P

SOURCE

A china medallion made by Wedgwood in about 1790. He wanted to see an end to slavery. The words on it say 'Am I not a man and a brother?'

I believe that all people are God's children. Africans are not different. They should not be slaves. We ask American slave owners to free them.

A Quaker
[A member of a Christian group that began in the 1650s.]

We believe that slavery is cruel and wicked. I am ashamed that there are over 20,000 black people in England today [1772]. Many are slaves. The courts have agreed to ban slavery in England.

An Evangelical
[A member of a group from the Church of England. They wanted to get rid of bad and evil things.]

William Wilberforce
[An Evangelical.]

I am fighting in Parliament for the ending of slavery [1807]. It has been hard. A lot of people make money from the slave trade. I say we make enough money now from other goods. We don't need to buy and sell human beings!

Q

SOURCE

I had never seen people being so extremely cruel to others. An African asks you to follow your God who says, 'Treat others as you would like them to treat you.'

From the lifestory of Olaudah Equiano. He was once a slave. He came to England and wrote his story. He also made speeches against slavery. Many people were shocked when he told them his story.

In **1807** the slave trade (buying slaves) was banned. In **1833** slavery (keeping slaves) was banned in the British Empire. By this time, the USA was not ruled by Britain. So slavery continued there until 1867.

Handwritten speech text in image:
By G—d that's too bad if he had taken her to bed to him it would ben enough. Split me I'm almost sick of this Black Business.

My Eyes Jack our Gorls at Wapping are never flogged for their mostely

Dam me if I like it I have a good mind to let go?

This cartoon was drawn by someone who wanted an end to the slave trade. It shows the cruel treatment of slaves on the 'Middle Passage'.

Question

People in the 18th and 19th centuries had different attitudes to the slave trade. Look at the list of people below. Try to match each person with the list of views about the slave trade. In **each case** try to add a sentence of your own to explain their reasons for their views on the slave trade.

A plantation owner	will be out of a job if the Liverpool ships do not get back from America with their cargo of raw cotton.
A Lancashire cotton factory worker	may be shocked by the slave trade but he does not think it is his job to make changes.
A Member of Parliament	believes that Africans are God's people and should be treated as equals.
A Quaker	is not able to grow his crops without slave labour.

4.1 Politics in Britain and Abroad

Who had the power in Britain in 1750?

The **King** still had some power. He could choose his own **prime minister**. He and his followers became the **government**. They sat in **Parliament**. They had to rule the country with the king. But the king decided what actions (**policies**) the government would take. If the government disagreed with the king he would ask someone else to be prime minister.

Parliament had more power than in earlier times (for example, in the Middle Ages). It could refuse to do what the king wanted. But this never happened. MPs were rich landowners from the upper classes. They were usually on the king's side.

MPs and voters

The **middle-class** (businessmen, doctors, lawyers) were not MPs in 1750. They had no say in how the country was run. But at least they could vote. **Working-class** people had no say at all. They could not even vote.

So the king and the upper classes held all the power in 1750.

Change on the horizon

This was not going to last for much longer. Two events abroad began to give ordinary people in Britain the idea that they had rights. If they stood up for themselves, they could win.

The King

The Prime Minister

The Government

Parliament

The House of Commons | The House of Lords

The Electorate

The Rest of the Population

The political system in Britain in 1750.

A

SOURCE

All men were made equal. God has given to everyone the right to life, freedom and happiness. Governments are there to make sure that everyone has these rights. If a government does not do this then the people have the right to remove it. Then they can replace it with another government that will protect them.

From the American Declaration of Independence, 1776.

The American Revolution 1775

The thirteen colonies in America belonged to Britain. They were ruled by the king and parliament. They also had to pay taxes to Britain. They thought that if they paid taxes they should have MPs to represent them. The king did not agree. Taxes got higher and higher. So in 1775 the Americans decided to fight for their freedom. They won. In 1783 the United States of America came into being.

The French Revolution 1789

The French king, Louis XVI, kept all the power in France to himself. A lot of people in France were unhappy with this. In 1789 poor people were starving. So on 14 July, a mob attacked the **Bastille**, a prison in Paris. The king was removed from the throne. Louis, his wife and many of the upper classes in France were later beheaded. The British government was afraid that there might also be a revolution in Britain. So Britain fought a war with the French from 1793 until 1815. But many people admired the Americans and the French because they had fought for their rights.

B SOURCE

A cartoon showing Tom Paine causing trouble for the British government.

Questions

Read Source A.

1 a Why should all people be equal?
 b What should the government do?
 c What should the people do if the government is bad?

Look at Page 70.
2 If you were one of the rest of the population in 1750, what sort of things would you complain about? Make a list.

C SOURCE

The execution of Louis XVI, 21 January 1793.

4.2 Power to the People (1)

The changes in industry affected people in different ways. Some people made a lot of money from industry and trade. But many people were worse off after the changes.

Protest

Workers needed laws to protect them. But the MPs only looked after the better off people who voted for them. So the poor turned to protest and violence to draw attention to their complaints.

The Luddites (1811–12)

The Luddites were machine breakers. They broke into factories in the North and Midlands. They smashed the new machines that were putting skilled men out of work.

The Swing Riots (1830)

In the south of England, farm workers destroyed new farm machinery. This was putting people out of work. Families were starving.

A Luddite attack, 1812. The government treated machine breakers harshly.

A painting of the House of Commons in 1800. The MPs were almost all rich landowners. They were afraid that the workers might start a revolution.

B

SOURCE

A cartoon from 1819. It shows the Peterloo Massacre.

'Votes for all' and the Peterloo Massacre

Some middle-class men said that MPs would listen to the workers' complaints if they were voters. So the workers began to demand the right to vote.

In 1819 Henry 'Orator' Hunt held a meeting at St Peter's Fields in Manchester. He was going to speak about the right to vote. Whole families came. The government sent soldiers to stop the meeting, saying it was against the law. The soldiers rode into the crowd. Eleven people were killed. Four hundred people were wounded.

Questions

Read **Protest**.
1 Draw a poster to show the complaints of the workers and the changes they wanted.

Look at Source C.
2 **a** Who went to the meeting?
  b How does the artist show the government had no sympathy for the workers?
  c Whose side is the artist on? Explain your answer.

In 1820 there was a plot to get rid of the government. It was called the Cato Street Conspiracy. The leaders were executed.

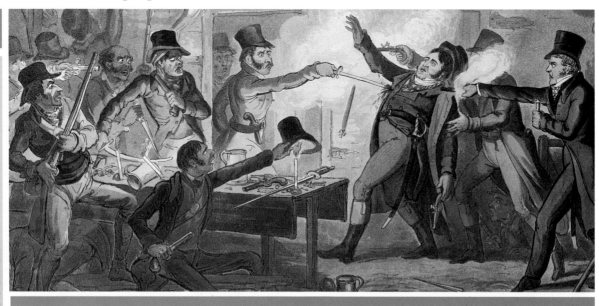

4.3 Power to the People (2)

By 1830 factories and towns were changing Britain. But the way that Britain was governed had not changed.

Why did government need to change?

1 Only a very few people could vote.
2 The changes in Britain had made the voting rules out of date. Tiny villages had MPs but large, new industrial towns like Manchester had none.
3 There was no one in the House of Commons to speak for people in the industrial areas. MPs were farmers and landowners
4 Voting was not done in secret. Voters were bribed (given money) to vote for people who wanted to become MPs.

By 1830 there were public meetings demanding change. There were even riots. Some MPs were afraid that there might be a revolution like the one in France. The House of Commons had to be changed. It had to represent more of the British people.

A An election was held for the borough of Finsbury. All those who did not have the right to vote were told to leave or they would be sent to prison. No one took any notice. The name of each candidate was read out. The voters for each one had to raise their hands Many people (including boys) who were not voters put up their hands. Mr Wakeley and Mr Grant were the winners. But the other candidates did not agree. They said that the voters must be checked to make sure that they all had the right to vote. This was done. Five days later, Mr Grant and Mr Spankie were declared the winners.

SOURCE

A description of a public election. This was in 'The Observer' newspaper in December 1832.

B

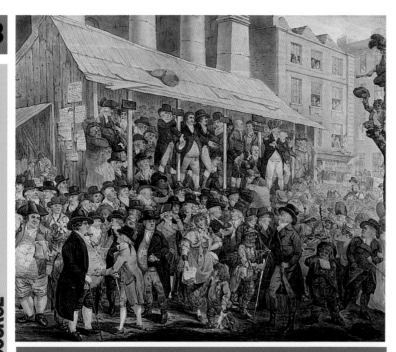

SOURCE

An election scene in London in 1796.

A cartoon from 1832. It shows how the Reform Act took 86 MPs away from very small places and gave them to the new industrial towns.

The path to reform

In 1831 there were two parties in Parliament – the **Whigs** and the **Tories.** The Whigs wanted change. Lord Grey, their leader, asked the Commons to make these changes. But the House of Lords refused to agree. The people were very angry. There were riots in Bristol that lasted for three days. Grey tried again. This time the Lords were too afraid to refuse.

The Great Reform Act 1832

This new law tried to share out the number of MPs more fairly. Places where the population was very small lost their MPs. Large industrial towns now had MPs.

Disappointment

Working people hoped that the new law would give them the vote. But it was only given to middle-class people in the towns. So the demand for change went on.

Questions

Read **Why did government need to change**?

1 Complete these sentences. Government had to change because _____ had changed. Tiny villages had _____MPs. Manchester had _____.

Read **The Great Reform Act 1832** and **Disappointment**.

2 a What changed after 1832?
  b What stayed the same after 1832 ?

D

The 1832 Reform Act did nothing for the workers. There were 400,000 new voters. But these were factory owners and businessmen.

From 'Britain since 1700' by R. J. Cootes, 1968.

E The 1832 Reform Act was very important. Many other reforms followed [laws to do with working in factories and coalmines]. Acts were passed later to give more and more working men the vote. It also made sure that there was not a revolution in England.

From a book by C. P. Hill, written in 1968.

4.4 Power to the People (3)

After 1850, working men found another way to get a fair deal. They joined together in trade unions.

Early trade unions

There had been trade unions before 1850. But employers did not like them. They thought the unions encouraged workers to cause trouble by going on strike.

Trade unions are accepted

By the 1850s skilled workers, like engineers and shipbuilders, had set up New Model Unions. Employers accepted these unions because they talked about their complaints. They did not just go on strike. They had a large number of members.

Votes for the working class

Politicians began to accept that some working men ought to be able to vote. So new laws were passed in Parliament:

1867: The vote was given to better-off workers in towns.

1884: The vote was given to farm workers.

But what about the rest?

Trade unions for the unskilled

The rest were unskilled workers, like dockers. In the 1880s they also joined new unions. But they went on strike to make their employers raise wages. By 1900 these unions had two million members.

A SOURCE

Loss of tools	£ 5
Sickness	£ 0.12s
Funeral	£ 12
Accident	£100

Union help for skilled workers.

B SOURCE

1884

| Population | 30 million |
| Voters | 5,700,000 |

There were still a lot of people who could not vote.

C SOURCE

A New Model Union membership card from 1870.

We need our working hours cut.

Then, no one will be sick or unemployed.

Said by the leader of the Gas Workers Union in 1889.

Questions

Copy out the statements below. Put 'T' for true or 'F' for false beside each one:

a By 1850 all workers belonged to a union.

b Unions looked after their members.

c Dockers were unskilled workers.

d Farm workers were given the vote in 1884.

e Most men and women had the vote by 1900.

f Keir Hardie was the first leader of the Labour Party.

Better times for working people?

After 1867 MPs had to listen to the complaints of working class voters. Slowly, laws were passed to make their lives better.

Working-class MPs began to sit in the House of Commons. One of these was Keir Hardie. He became the first leader of the Labour Party when it was formed in 1903.

But there was still a long way to go. Some men still did not have the vote. Women did not have the vote at all.

'The British Beehive', drawn in 1840. It shows British society in the 19th century.

A PENNY POLITICAL PICTURE FOR THE PEOPLE, WITH A FEW WORDS UPON PARLIAMENTARY REFORM BY THEIR OLD FRIEND, GEORGE CRUIKSHANK

4.5 Gladstone and Disraeli

William Ewart Gladstone

Gladstone was born in Liverpool in 1809. He went to Eton and then to Oxford University. He was a Christian. He tried to carry out his Christain beliefs as an MP.

Some important dates in his career:

1832	He became a Tory MP.
1843	He was made President of the Board of Trade.
1846	He joined the Liberals.
1852–55 } 1859–65 }	He was the Chancellor of the Exchequer.
1868–74 } 1880–85 } 1886 } 1892–94 }	He was the Prime Minister.

Gladstone's achievements:

- He gave more working men the vote.
- He improved schools so that poorer children could have more education.
- He tried to give peace and more freedom to Ireland.

'The Grand Old Man'

Gladstone died in 1898. He was remembered for his hard work and long speeches!

Benjamin Disraeli

Disraeli was born in 1804 into a rich Jewish family. He became a Christian.

Some important dates in his career:

1846	He became important in the Tory Party.
1852 } 1858–9 } 1866–8 } 1868 }	He was Chancellor of the Exchequer.
1874–80	He was Prime Minister.

Disraeli's achievements:

- He gave working men in the towns the vote in 1867.
- He passed some laws to make working and living conditions better.
- He made the British Empire bigger. He made Queen Victoria the Empress of India. He sent the army to Africa and kept the British lands there.
- He did not think that the Irish should be free.

Lord Beaconsfield

Queen Victoria liked Disraeli. She gave him the title of Lord Beaconsfield in 1876. He died in 1881.

A

Cartoons of Gladstone (top) and Disraeli (botto

Prime Ministers with a difference

Gladstone was a very honest and serious man. He cared about people who were unfairly treated. He always tried to do what was right and good. People nicknamed him the 'Grand Old Man'. **Disraeli** was a lively and colourful character. He did things that seemed to be right at the time. He was very popular. People nicknamed him 'Dizzie'.

The 'Eastern Question'

This is a good example of how Gladstone and Disraeli were different. The 'Eastern Question' was all about Turkey and the Turkish (Ottoman) Empire. In the 19th century Britain was afraid that Russia was becoming too big. Only the Turkish Empire stopped Russia taking over more land. But some countries in the Ottoman Empire wanted to be free of Turkish rule. What should Britain do? Disraeli said that the Turkish Empire must not break up because it stopped Russia from getting bigger. He felt that this was the most important thing at the time. **Gladstone** did not agree. He knew that the Sultan of Turkey was a very cruel ruler. He believed that the people of the Empire should be free.

Questions

Look back over pages 78 and 79.

1 Write down two headings: **Similarities** and **Differences**. Make a list of the things that were the **same** about Gladstone and Disraeli and the things that were **different**.

2 If you could travel back in time and meet Gladstone and Disraeli, which of the two do you think you would like the better? Explain your answer using what you have learned about them.

This 1870 cartoon from 'Punch' shows Gladstone (right) and Disraeli (left) as two very different people.

B

SOURCE

4.6 Education

In 1750 poor people's children went to work. Only rich people's children were educated. Education cost money. Poor people could not afford it.

Schools for the rich

The sons of the rich went to public schools, like Eton, or to grammar schools. They went on to university, usually Oxford or Cambridge. Girls were mostly taught at home. They were brought up to expect to marry a rich man. Some girls were allowed into public schools after 1850.

Schools for the poor

In some places poor children went to charity schools. Even these cost about a penny for each lesson. Children were taught very simple reading and writing. There were also dame schools. These were usually run by women in their own homes. They sometimes taught very little at all. From 1780 there were Sunday schools.

Church schools

More schools were needed as the population grew. The Church of England (in 1811) and other churches, like the Methodists (in 1814), set up schools.

A

SOURCE

I didn't learn anything useful at Harrow. We only learnt to recite Latin. We were bullied by older boys. They sen us out to buy beer. If we were caught we were caned.

Memories of going to Harrow School in 1848.

Students at Oxford and Cambridge enjoyed themselves most of the time. They spent more time having fun than studying.

B

SOURCE

There were 170 boys in the class. There was no History or Geography. The Bible was the only book in use.

The teacher taught a small number of boys. Then these boys went and taught the rest.

From a report by an inspector on a church school.

C

SOURCE

D

SOURCE

The poor should not be educated. They will expect more. They will not do as they are told.

From a speech against schools for the poor.

E

SOURCE

If we want to be a great power in the world, we must educate more of the people. If we want to be a rich country, our people must be educated.

Said by an MP who wanted schools for the poor.

G

SOURCE

A picture of a dame school painted about 1850. Dame schools were often just places where children were looked after, not taught.

The government and schools

The government began to help by giving money to the church schools. Then, in 1871, the first Education Act set up State schools. But it was not until 1880 that a law said children under ten years had to go to school. And it was not until 1891 that education was free.

F

SOURCE

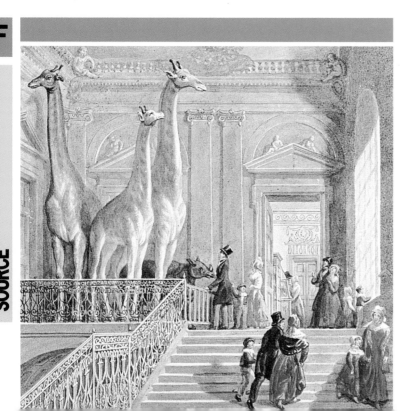

Questions

Read **Schools for the rich** and **Schools for the poor**.
1 Make two headings: **Rich children** and **Poor children**. Under each heading say what kind of schools were available to children.

Read **The government and schools**.
2 Finish the sentences below:
The 1871 Education Act _____.
The 1880 Education Act _____.
The 1891 Education Act _____.

The British Museum in 1845. People went to museums or evening classes to learn about things they had not learnt at school.

4.7 Connections – Politics and the Industrial Revolution

You have already seen how the changes in farming, industry and transport were linked together. You have been learning in this part of the book about the beginning of changes in **politics** (things to do with government). Some working people joined together to help these changes to take place. These changes are also linked to the changes in industry and transport. Look at the diagram below:

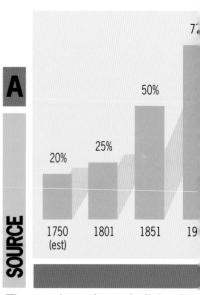

SOURCE A

The number of people living in towns (shown in percentages).

20% 25% 50%

1750 (est)　1801　1851　19

In the 19th century there were more and more people.

More people working in industry instead of farming.

More people living in dirty towns and working in bad conditions.

Working people beginning to think they should have a better life.

Working people wanted MPs to represent them and they wanted to be able to vote.

Protest Working people began to make demands. They thought of themselves as a group.

Better transport and communications. Ideas could spread more quickly. People could travel.

SOURCE B

If millions of people join together we will win!

William Lovett, the Chartist leader, speaking in 1840.

SOURCE C

Every industry came to a stop. The docks were full of ships that could not be loaded or unloaded. The Dockers' Union have done this. Other workers can see what they can do if they join together.

The effects of a dockers' strike, desribed in a newspaper in 188

cartoonist shows what he thinks of the 'Six Acts' aws to stop calls for reform).

A cartoon by Rowlandson, 1819, showing news sheets being sold in the streets.

Questions

Look at page 82.
1 Copy the diagram. Colour in the links of the chain. Choose a different colour for each of the following:
   farming
   industry
   transport
   politics.

2 Write a few sentences explaining how these four things are linked together.

A cartoon in 'Punch', 1843. It shows the differences between the rich and the poor.

4.8 Chartism: A Study in Depth

This depth study looks more closely at how working people joined together to make their lives better. This group called themselves Chartists. You will find the answers to these questions:

- Who were the Chartists ?
- Why did they want changes?
- What changes did the Chartists want?
- What did the government think of the Chartists?
- How did the Chartists try to get change?
- What did the Chartists achieve?

Who were the Chartists?

The Chartists got their name because they supported the **People's Charter (1838)**. This was a list of six changes that the people wanted. Their leaders were **William Lovett**, a cabinet maker and **Francis Place**, a tailor. These men tried to persuade working-class people to join together. They believed that it was the only way to bring about change.

Why did the Chartists want change?

As you have learned already, since 1750, the lives of working people had changed greatly. They now lived and worked in horrible conditions. Britain had become very rich, but most workers were still poor. Some skilled workers had lost their jobs because of the new machines.

If the price of wheat went up, working people struggled to survive because they could not afford bread. Nothing was done to help them. There was no one to speak for them.

Lovett and Place said working people should be able to vote. They needed MPs in Parliament to look after them. Britain had changed so Parliament must also change. But MPs did not want to change.

A

SOURCE

You need to vote to get the basic things of life – good food, clothes and a house for your family. A working man should not have to work so hard that he becomes ill. He should have enough money to live a good life.

A Chartist in Lancashire tells the workers what having the vote will do for them.

B

SOURCE

C

SOURCE

Chartist leaders: Feargus O'Conn▸ (top) and William Lovett (bottom)

What changes did the Chartists want?

In 1832 Parliament had made changes (look back at page 85). But working-class people were no better off. So their leaders drew up the **People's Charter** in 1838. It set out six demands. You can see these in Source E.

What did the government think of the Chartists?

MPs did not like working-class people meeting together in large numbers to demand change. They were still afraid that there might be a revolution in Britain. They did not want to change Parliament any more.

(look back at page 85)

D

SOURCE

Let all the working classes join together. Let us find out about our rights from books Let us show people that wages are low and conditions are bad. Then MPs will agree there must be change.

From a speech by William Lovett in 1836.

E

SOURCE

The Six Points of the PEOPLE'S CHARTER

1 Every man of 21 years of age should have a vote.
2 Voting should be done in secret. This would stop bribery.
3 People should not have to own property to be an MP.
4 MPs should be paid. Working people could then afford to be MPs.
5 Voting districts [constituencies] should have equal numbers of voters.
6 There should be a new parliament every year. This would stop MPs breaking promises.

This poster shows what the Chartists wanted. They thought about including votes for women but decided not to add this point.

SOURCE

Many women became Chartists. They joined in the campaign. Some started their own groups. Male Chartists agreed that women must have the vote as well as men.

From 'The Chartists', by Dorothy Thompson, in 1986.

Questions

1 Draw your own Chartist poster showing the six points.

2 What did MPs think about the Chartists?

Standing order of the House. All members, not being able to stand or sit, are ordered to lie under the table.

How did the Chartists try to get change?

Some Chartists wanted to win by using peaceful methods.

1 They held **rallies** (big meetings) in cities such as Birmingham, Liverpool and Leeds. This was to get the ordinary people to join in large numbers.
2 They drew up a **petition** in 1839 and took it to Parliament. It was signed by 1,250,000 people. But Parliament voted against the Chartists.

What next?

Some Chartists wanted to use force to get what they wanted. One of these was **Feargus O'Connor**. Another was **Bronterre O'Brien**.

This is a cartoon from the time. It is called 'A Commons Scene'. It shows what some people thought the Commons would be like if the Chartists got what they wanted.

H

I do not want to use force. But if we do not succeed we must use violence. It will be the right thing to do if it wins us our freedom.

From a speech made by Feargus O'Connor.

The Newport Rising 1839

The government was afraid that the Chartists might become violent. So they sent 6,000 soldiers to the North of England. They were there to let the Chartists know what would happen if they caused trouble.

Trouble came in Newport, South Wales. Chartists there became angry because the soldiers kept showing off with their guns. Also some Chartist leaders were being kept prisoners in the Westgate Hotel, Newport. Their followers decided to try to free them. They were led by John Frost. About 5,000 Chartists attacked the hotel on the night of 3–4 November 1839. But the soldiers were ready for them. They fired on the Chartists. Twenty men were killed. One hundred were arrested.

I

SOURCE

A cartoon showing a Chartist getting ready to fight. The coal scuttle and dish were not likely to protect him much from the guns of the army!

J

SOURCE

The Chartist attack on the Westgate Hotel, Newport. There are a lot of Chartists but they are not all armed with guns. A lot of them only have sticks.

Hunger and unemployment 1842

Working-class people supported the Chartists when times were bad for them. After 1839 food prices fell. So things got better. Fewer people followed the Chartists. But in 1842 hardship hit them yet again. Once more they were happy to join the Chartists.

Feargus O'Connor

By 1842 O'Connor was the main Chartist leader. He owned a newspaper called the **Leeds Northern Star**. He wrote articles for his paper to get more support.

The Second Petition 1842

This had 3,317,000 signatures and was six miles long! It was carried to London by 50 workers. A two mile long procession of workers followed. But this made no difference. Parliament still said no to change.

K Handloom weavers here are Chartists because they hate the new machines. They also support violence. Some even call for the mills to be burned. Factory workers are different. They support peaceful methods.

SOURCE

From the writings of John Cook, who visited Lancashire in 1842.

The Chartists take their 1842 petition to Parliament.

L

SOURCE

More violence

Workers were disappointed that the second petition was thrown out by Parliament. In Lancashire, cotton spinners went on strike. Over 9,000 met on Mottram Moor near Manchester. They wanted to make Parliament accept the six points of the Charter.

The 'plug plot'

Not all workers joined in the strike. So those who were on strike took the plugs out of the boilers of the steam engines in factories that were still working! The Chartist leaders wanted all workers everywhere to come out on strike (**a general strike**). But not enough workers would join this protest.

Many of the strikers were punished. Seventy-nine were **transported** (carried off) to Australia. The strike did not last long after that. In 1843, things got better again for the workers.

A split in the ranks?

Once again Chartist fortunes fell. To make things worse, the Chartists disagreed amongst themselves. Some leaders still wanted to protest peacefully. Others thought that they would not get anything unless they were violent.

Questions

1 Why did some Chartists think that violence was the only way to win and others wanted peaceful protest?

2 Draw a poster to persuade Chartists **either** to use violence **or** to use peaceful methods.

This shows O'Connorville. It was a kind of 'new town' started by O'Connor in an attempt to improve the living conditions of workers. Another 'new town' was built near Witney in Oxfordshire.

One more try

In 1847–8 food prices and unemployment went up again. In 1848 the Chartists decided to take a **third petition** to Parliament. This time they said that 5,700,000 people had signed it and that 500,000 Chartists would take it to the Houses of Parliament.

London was prepared for trouble. Queen Victoria left London. Thousands of soldiers and special constables were ready to protect the city. But on the day only 20,000 people met on Kennington Common. They were not allowed to march to the Houses of Parliament so they went home. The petition was taken to Parliament by Feargus O'Connor. Again the demands were turned down. Little more was heard of the Chartists.

What did the Chartists achieve?

It looks as though the Chartists had failed. Working people did not need Chartism anymore. Life was getting better for them. Why was this?
- After 1848 there were more jobs.
- Wages and working conditions got better.
- Food came to Britain from abroad. It was cheap because the government did not tax it any more.
- Workers began to help themselves. They joined trade unions. They joined together to open shops to sell cheap goods (co-operative societies). They also started friendly societies to help each other if they fell on hard times.

But the Chartists did not fail completely:
- All of their demands, except a new parliament each year, later became law.
- They drew attention to the problems of working people. This helped to bring about change.
- They showed working people that things could get better for them if they joined together.

SOURCE N

The MP for Nottingham [Feargus O'Connor] said that there were 5,706,000 names on the petition. When these were looked at closely, there were only 1,975,496. Many of the names were made up. On some pages there were the names of Queen Victoria, the Duke of Wellington and other famous people.

From a House of Commons report, 1848.

SOURCE O

A 'Punch' cartoon. It is making fun of the petition with all its false signatures.

A drawing of the Chartist meeting on Kennington Common in 1848.

Questions

1 Below are the important dates in the story of the Chartists. Find out what happened in each of these years:
1838 (Page 85)
1839 (Page 86)
1839 (Page 87)
1842 (Page 89)
1848 (Page 90)

Now draw a **Chartist timeline**.

2 Use your timeline and the diagram to tell the story of the Chartists.

3 Did working people **really** care about being able to vote?

4 Copy the diagram below, but make it much bigger. Write one or two sentences in each box to answer the question.

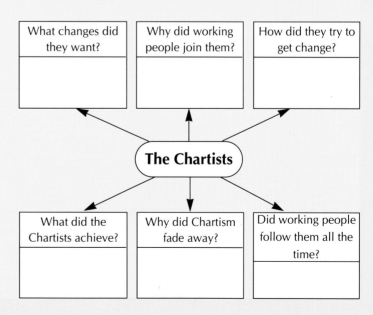

What changes did they want?	Why did working people join them?	How did they try to get change?

The Chartists

What did the Chartists achieve?	Why did Chartism fade away?	Did working people follow them all the time?

5.1 Britain in 1900 – So far from 1750

Expansion

By 1900 Britain had the biggest empire in the world. People left Britain to begin a new life in parts of this empire. **But** other countries were jealous of Britain's empire, especially Germany. This would lead to war.

Trade

Britain still exported more goods than any other country. These were carried in British ships. The ships were powered first by sail, then steam. **But** other countries were catching up. And other countries were starting to discover new technology first.

Population

There were more people to feed and clothe. There were more people to work. By 1900 anaesthetics and antiseptics were helping people to survive operations. **But** there was still no cure for many diseases.

This picture, called 'Work', was painted in 1863. The Victorians admired people who worked hard.

Industry

By 1900 Britain had changed from a farming country to an industrial country. Cotton mills, iron and steel works, steam power, machinery and the railways all changed Britain. **But** industry also brought bad housing, overcrowded towns, long working hours and poor wages. These were only just being improved by 1900.

Government

By 1900 the Prime Minister and parliament were more powerful than Queen Victoria. This seemed like the people were getting more power. **But** women and some working men still did not have the vote.

Leisure

By 1900 people had a little more money and time to enjoy themselves:

going by train to the seaside
watching the travelling circus
nights out at the music halls
days at the races or cricket matches
watching a local football team.

New technology

By 1900 those with money could:

send a telegram to America
buy a vacuum cleaner, telephone or washing machine
have gas lights in the home
drive a petrol engine car
live on a street lit by gas or electricity.

B

SOURCE

TOO MUCH OF A GOOD THING

EVERY VARIETY OF PLEASURE RESORT.

PARKS & PLAYGROUNDS
RIVER-SIDE
COUNTRY-SIDE
SEASIDE
PALACES & GARDENS.

The London Underground. This poster dates from 1910. The Underground opened in 1863.

Questions

1 Copy the sentence below that best describes Britain in 1900:

Britain had changed completely by 1900.

Britain had changed a lot by 1900, but some things had not changed.

Britain had not changed at all by 1900.

2 Explain your choice. Use the information on pages 92 and 93.

5.2 Britain in 1900 – So close to today

Our inheritance from the past

Many things about our lives today remind us of Britain from 1750 to 1900. Some of the buildings from this time are still used – for example, the Houses of Parliament. In the north of England some of the textile factories are still standing. These are now used for other purposes. You can still see coal mines. Canals, bridges and railways remind us of the great engineers. Cars, aeroplanes and bicycles are part of our lives today; they were all invented in the 19th century.

The people of Britain

The population started to grow rapidly in the 19th century. Today, 55 million people live in Britain. Some of these people came from countries that were once part of the British Empire. The Empire has now gone but Britain is still a multi-cultural country.

Britain and its government

Britain is still made up of England, Scotland and Wales, but now only Northern Ireland. We still have a monarch. But in the 19th century we saw how power passed completely to Parliament. Everyone (not just men!) over 18 years can now vote. People are protected by laws at home and at work.

n search of the past

oday, people are very curious about this period in our
ast. You can relive these times in museums such as Wigan
ier in Lancashire, Beamish in County Durham and Blists
ill, near Coalbrookdale in Shropshire.

earching for the past helps us to see what we owe to our
ncestors. It also shows us how our lives have moved on
nce then. Often **our** lives are better because of **their**
xperiences.

Questions

1 Make a list of all the things on
these two pages that we have
today but come from
1750–1900.

2 Think of as many things as
you can that we have
changed.

3 Do you think that the changes
have made things better?